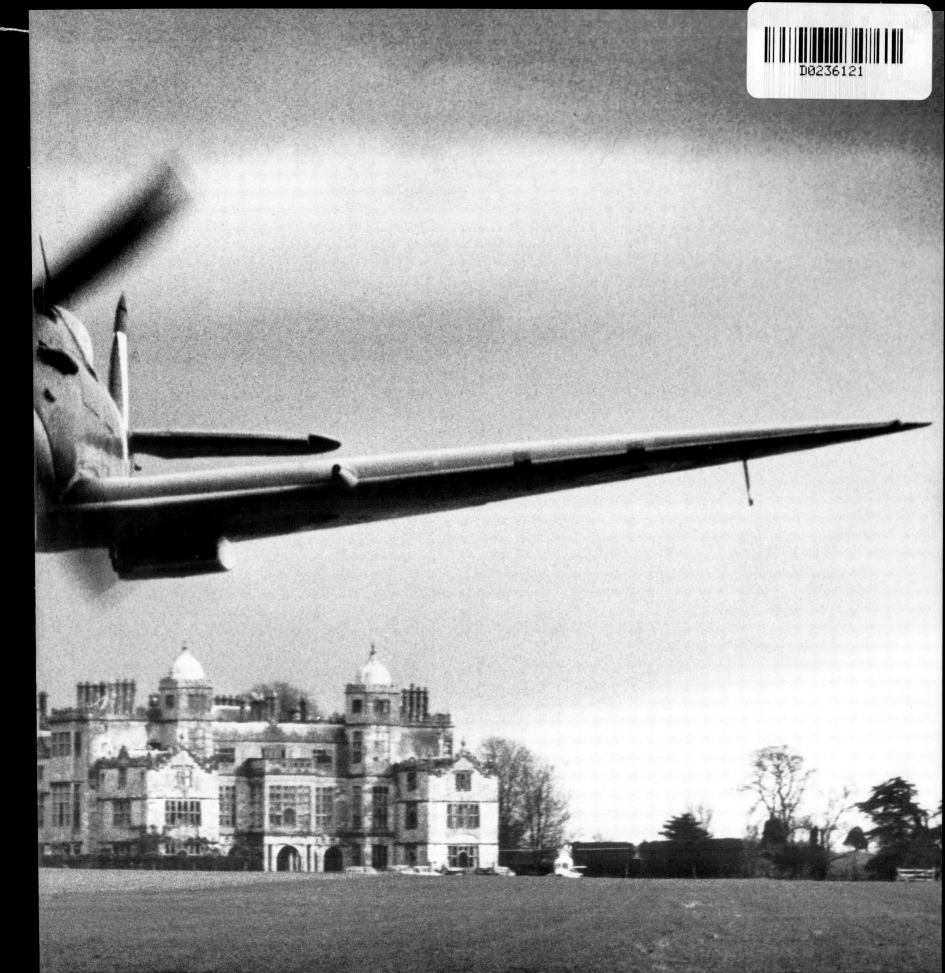

How they made
PIECE ⊙F CAKE

How they made
PIECE ⊙F CAKE

ROBERT EAGLE and HERBIE KNOTT

LLWT

Boxtree

First published in 1988 by Boxtree Limited

Text © copyright 1988 London Weekend Television
Photographs © copyright 1988 Herbie Knott

Designed by Groom and Pickerill
Typeset by Bookworm Typesetting, Manchester.
Printed and bound in Great Britain by
Butler and Tanner Ltd., Frome and London.

for Boxtree Limited
36, Tavistock Street,
London WC2E 7PB.

British Library Cataloguing in Publication Data

Eagle, Robert
    How they made Piece of cake
    1. Great Britain. television programmes
    791.45'0941

ISBN 1-85283-239-8

CONTENTS

FIRING UP

The beginnings of *Piece of Cake*

ROBERT EAGLE

The sight of three little Spitfires flying aerobatics over the English coast stirs all sorts of emotions. The pleasure is instinctive; it makes your pulse beat faster and your heart leap up in sympathy to the elegant little aircraft.

Two thousand feet up, the aeroplanes look brave and frail; even when they dive down to just ten feet above the ground and zoom towards you at 250 miles per hour, they look too beautiful to be threatening.

The loveliness of the aeroplane makes you forget that it was designed to fight and kill. With its slim, compact airframe and the unmistakable pointed curve of its elliptical wings, its beauty conceals its true purpose. A Messerschmitt, Zero or Hurricane looks like a killing machine, but the Spitfire is a work of art, a pleasure to ear and eye.

These feelings are of course tinged with more than a dash of patriotic pride; more than any other aircraft the Spitfire remains in British minds as the machine which saved the nation in its darkest hour. And its name is just as potent for the many millions who were born long after that dark hour had passed.

Piece of Cake is a television drama. It is about people; their characters and conflicts are the essence of the series, and the aircraft are really only props to the drama. Despite their charisma, they could not be allowed to steal the show. Many young actors have established their names with their performances in *Piece of Cake*. Technically, too, *Piece of Cake* is an innovative production: the first British television series to use a new kind of 35mm film format, combined with extensive use of new state of the art computer effects and animation.

But you should have done it with Hurricanes!

You are never going to please everyone. Six months before the series was even broadcast, one of Herbie Knott's photographs in the *Independent* had correspondents reaching for their pens in high dudgeon to write letters to the editor and producers. Herbie's photograph showed the squadron scrambling to their Spitfires in the winter mud at Charlton Park, the Wiltshire location which served as our French airfield. What annoyed the letter writers was that we were using Spitfires at all. Hurricanes, we were severely told, were what we should be using for a drama set in France during that time,

Tail-chasing at Friston.

Right *Spitfire MH434 takes off from Friston.*

Below *Nick Grace in Me 109 chased round the cliffs by Hoof Proudfoot in Mk I Spitfire.*

First sortie for the cast, Charlton Park, February 1988.

and if we could not get Hurricanes we should be using model Hurricanes.

The correspondents were right about the Hurricanes. Indeed Derek Robinson's novel on which the television series was based had featured Hurricanes and Hurricanes were what we would have dearly loved to use. The reason we did not use them is very simple: there were only three flyable Hurricanes in the world, two owned by the RAF and one in a Canadian museum, hardly enough to make a squadron, even if we could have got them all together and working at the same time. The RAF also restricts the number of hours it allows its historic

aircraft to be flown.

In retrospect, it was a blessing that we had to turn to Spitfires for *Piece of Cake*. Although there are precious few of these aircraft, we were always able to get at least four in the air, sometimes five, and they were operated by private owners and pilots, who flew their aircraft with breathtaking skill and bravura to match the daring of the young pilots half a century ago.

Piece of Cake, the novel, had taken Derek Robinson four years to research and write. He is a painstaking writer; though the novel is a work of fiction, many of the incidents were inspired by actual events which occurred during the first twelve months of World War Two. He had read just about every available memoir about the period and had personally interviewed scores of former pilots. The novel was not intended to be a conventional piece of hero worship. It drew much of its own drama from the disputes and debates which arose when the 'Phoney War' of 1939 and early 1940 came to an end and the British were pushed into the sea at Dunkirk. What had impressed producer Andrew Holmes about the novel were its characters and its strong pictorial quality; so many of the incidents leap colourfully into the mind's eye.

The novel was adapted for television by Leon Griffiths, best known as the originator of *Minder*, one of the British television's most successful and long running series. Though he had to reduce much of the action and lose a few of the characters from Robinson's long novel, his script brought out the best qualities of the original story: its pace, its humour, and its unconventional but honest appraisal of the qualities of those fighter pilots.

'Having read just five pages of the script I realised it had enormous potential,' recalls Ian Toynton, *Piece*

Marginal conditions. Ray Hanna over Gloucestershire.

Right *Spitfires over Wiltshire.*

Below *Between takes, Friston.*

of Cake's director. 'I loved its originality and its unpredictability, and I could believe in its characters.'

The production called for a large cast of young, untried actors, an unusual variety of locations and visual effects, not to mention the flying of old aircraft in combat sequences which would put men and machines at full stretch.

Piece of Cake was a drama, not an aviation documentary, and it was essential that the script should be brought to life by the actors and direction rather than by extravagant bursts of aeronautical activity. As Ian Toynton pointed out: 'A plane is infinitely more interesting if you know who is flying it.' Finding the actors took longer than shooting the series. According to director Toynton, it was a pleasure to cast 'because there is such a great wealth of talented young actors in this country at the moment.' But there was a great deal of casting to do.

After detailed discussions with Toynton and Holmes about each character, casting director Marilyn Johnson came up with a list of over a hundred young actors to play ten of the principal parts. It took months to interview them all, draw up a shortlist of three for each part, then have them read the part at audition. Having made that selection, there were another *60* parts to cast. Actors for the role of Barton had to be sought in Australia, Hart was cast in the United States and possibles for Nicole and the male French roles had to be found in France.

On the set, it was extraordinary how easily the actors could be identified with their parts. If you knew the book,

Special effects department in action at Charlton Park. This replica Spitfire was rebuilt for the next location!

you could look at the cast and name the characters they were playing almost at a glance. Off the set, too, they retained their roles to an extraordinary degree. Richard Hope (Skull) and David Horovitch (Kellaway) became, not altogether to their liking, father confessor figures to the younger actors; Nat Parker (Flash) was usually the first to attract the female interest; Gerard O'Hare (Moran) crooned glum, satirical ballads; Neil Dudgeon (Cattermole) was the dry, scathing wit. The speed with which the cast formed itself into Hornet Squadron, on and off camera, took everyone by surprise.

The February morning when the pilots first appeared on set at Charlton Park, dressed as the officers of Hornet Squadron, was a moving moment for everyone. The moment did not last; by take two the pilots were slipping over and careering into each other in the mud.

The next big moment was when the first Spitfire landed; but for that we had to wait a few days.

Left *A wing and a prayer: waiting for the rain to clear at South Cerney. From left to right: Gerard O'Hare (Flip Moran), Linda Armstrong (make-up), Beryl Lerman (make-up), Peter Jessop (lighting cameraman), Ian Toynton (director), Leon Griffiths (screenwriter), Andrew Holmes (producer).*

Below *Tim Woodward ('Rex') with Toby ('Reilly'). South Cerney.*

WHY I WROTE PIECE OF CAKE

DEREK ROBINSON

Piece of Cake had its beginnings in 1940, when I was eight years old and the German Air Force began bombing Bristol, where I lived.

I had read a lot of Biggles books and even to my tiny mind there was a great difference between the blitz and Biggles. For a start, the books were very big on duels in the sky. Precious few duels in our sky in 1940. I have a vivid memory of watching a German bomber held in a cone of searchlights as it crossed the city, fresh beams of light collecting it when the old ones lost it, but I don't remember seeing it shot down; and in any case several dozen other German bombers were up there going about their business in the shelter of the night, scattering incendiaries like confetti. The battle seemed very lopsided to me. What's more, there was always a point and a purpose to the Biggles books; the plots made sense. Not much point to the Bristol blitz. I'm sure the Luftwaffe had its targets (docks and railway station) but at night the enemy's bomb-aimers were no better than ours, which meant they were often lucky to get their bombs within three miles of the target. So what impressed my eight-year-old mind was not so much the mess a 250-kg high-explosive bomb made of somebody's semi-detached up the road, total though that destruction was; the significant factor for me was the utterly *random* nature of such violence. It didn't matter where you lived, a bomb might come whistling out of the sky and destroy your home (and maybe you too) for no reason at all. With Biggles you always had a beginning, a middle, and an end (a happy end, too) whereas with your actual air raid you got a kind of furious chaos.

In September 1940 the Luftwaffe attacked the BAC (Bristol Airplane Company) factory at Filton. About 60 German bombers crossed the Channel, flew north over Dorset and Somerset without meeting any opposition, and reached Bristol at midday, still cruising in close formation. They made a shambles at BAC and then they flew home, having lost only a couple of planes. Now Biggles would never have allowed that to happen; but then (as I steadily realised) this wasn't a rattling good yarn I was living through. This was war, with its waste and confusion.

16

Above *They also served ... groundcrew at 'RAF Kingsmere' (South Cerney).*

Opposite *More than 50 soldiers from the Duke of Gloucester barracks at South Cerney took leave to work as extras on* Piece of Cake.

If there is any beauty in war it must lie in the aircraft. That beauty reached its peak in World War Two. The fighters, especially, were made for speed and performance, and when genius is at the drawing-board it creates a machine that makes your heart kick with joy as you watch it do its stuff. Every day I saw so many warplanes that I could identify them at a glance: the Hurricane and its big-chinned descendants, the Tempest and the Typhoon; the Beaufighter and the Beaufort; the sleek Mosquito with its shark's fin rudder; and God knows how many American types: the forked Lightning, the shark-mouthed Tomahawk, the barrel-bodied Thunderbolt, the jaunty-looking Mustang. And, of course, there was the Spitfire. To the very end – and they were making the Mark XXI when the war ended – there were always Spitfires in the sky. My boyhood was saturated with the sight and sound of those fighters and they entranced me in a way that modern fighters utterly fail to do. Today's fighter is a stupendous jet engine on wheels with a lot of ironmongery strapped underneath. Of course it goes fast; given that sort of thrust you could get anything up to Mach 2: a JCB, a Portaloo, Waterloo Bridge; anything. Beautiful it is not. It rockets about the sky, but it doesn't *fly*, not the way Spitfires and Hurricanes flew.

Okay. The war ends. Fast-forward now to 1951.

National Serviceman 2533409 AC2 Robinson is doing his basic square-bashing at RAF Padgate, near Warrington. Padgate was a huge camp, dedicated to training us recruits to leave a record of each step by creating a heel-shaped dent in the parade ground. ('Dig 'em in! Dig 'em in!' the drill corporals used to snarl.) I was still in love with aircraft and I was willing to learn peculiar non-aviation practices, such as how to strip and assemble a bren gun in the dark, if this led eventually to something connected with aeroplanes. And even a *gulag* like Padgate encouraged us to remember that the RAF was all about flying. On the walls were many charcoal portraits of wartime pilots.

This marked the beginning of my profoundly mixed feelings towards the RAF.

On the one hand I knew, more and more, from personal experience, that the RAF had its faults. It had, for instance, a very silly uniform. Battledress and best blue were ill-fitting and uncomfortably hot in summer. The trouser crease dissolved every time you marched into a mist. Each airman was issued with a complex harness of webbing that was a bitch to keep clean and that served no purpose except to be inspected. Because the RAF was hugely overmanned there was endless,

Background action. Groundcrew extras at work on real and replica Spitfires (South Cerney).

Below '*As long as I could watch a returning Spitfire beat up the field ...*' *(Charlton Park).*

Bottom *Mk XI Spitfire being refuelled from a WW2 period bowser (South Cerney).*

Opposite *Erk's eye view of Hornet Squadron.*

pointless, tedious make-work. For instance, the linoleum corridors in the ops block got polished by the morning watch so that when the afternoon watch arrived, it tramped along them in its tackety boots, thus providing themselves with something to do, and so on. Everyone was bored.

On the other hand, the more I saw of the RAF's aircraft and the men who flew them, the greater became my admiration for both. We were billeted

at Exeter Airport. The early 1950s were a time of international tension and the government recalled various groups of reservists to bolster the Services. That's how we came to have a bunch of World War Two pilots and a squadron of Spitfires attached to us.

They were marvellous blokes and they did our morale a power of good. They were, of course, far beyond the reach of normal discipline – they fell-in at parades wearing carpet slippers, pyjama tops and no hats – but they flew as they had flown in the war: as if they owned the sky. For those who were a bit rusty there was a Tiger Moth to practise in. One pilot used to fly the Moth over to our ops block and approach the radar aerial, which was as big as the side of a barn. As the aerial rotated, so he banked and turned with it, the Moth actually inside its radius, until he emerged and flew back the way he'd come. It was like watching a biplane tackle a revolving door.

The Exeter-to-Plymouth railway line ran nearby, much of it raised on an embankment because the ground was so marshy. The reservists used this as a low-flying area for Spitfires. They stooged about, waiting for an express to

appear, and then flew alongside the train, often below the level of the passengers.

For as long as those reservists were in business, and for as long as I heard their superb late-mark Spitfires being cartridge-started with a bang like the crack of doom and being run-up with a harsh, crackling roar that made conversation impossible even if you were inside a billet a hundred yards away, and for as long as I could watch a returning Spitfire beat up the field, or stand on its tail and drill spiralling holes in the sky, or merely stroll around

its landing circuit, wheels and flaps down like a beautiful bird feeling its way towards its roost – then I felt boundless pride.

My first novel was *Goshawk Squadron*. What prompted me to write it was the discovery that there was a great gulf between the popular legend of the chivalry of World War One air combat and the first-hand accounts of the pilots themselves.

Goshawk Squadron taught me the value of three other things, all of which I applied to *Piece of Cake*: history, humour, and 'stuff like Castrol'.

History means that *Goshawk* is built on a solid framework of fact. The war really did go the way I described it, with the German army launching a last desperate offensive in the West before the Americans could make a difference; which meant that the British and French were fighting *not to lose*, rather than to win: a tricky concept to get across to a pilot whose expectation of life was measured in weeks rather than months.

Humour is, for me, essential in fiction. I grew up on the likes of Wodehouse, Chandler and Waugh. I have read flying stories that lack all humour and are not, as a result, more serious; just less credible. Humour is an essential colour in the spectrum; remove it and you distort the picture. And from what I can see, aircrew usually managed to find something funny about war even at its most horrible. Perhaps the sheer relief of survival contributed to that.

'Stuff like Castrol' is a shorthand phrase for a ton of research, not only into the air war but into the whole history of the period: military and political and social. Castrol is a contraction of castor oil, which is what the product was first made of, and castor oil was a common engine lubricant in the RFC. I collected hundreds of bits of information like that. I couldn't find a use for 90 per cent (like the Ovaltine ad with a picture of an RFC pilot and

the promise that 'taken just before and after flight nothing can sustain Nerve and Body like a cup of Ovaltine') but the other 10 per cent proved very handy. It was the same when I researched the first year of World War Two for *Piece of Cake*.

The structure was obvious or so I thought. The Battle of Britain reached its climax in September 1940, just one year after war broke out. Twelve months meant twelve chapters, no more. Nice and neat. Piece of cake. But novels don't always go where you send them. Mine had its own idea about how it should be written. The first four chapters (September-December 1939) took 245 pages, and all the heavy action was yet to come! I scrapped the strict chapter-per-month format and told the story to do what it thought best. We telescoped the spring

Below *'Their response to almost everything was immediate, positive, direct ... they made friends easily.' (Pilots at play, South Cerney.)*

Opposite *'When war broke out most RAF pilots were in their early twenties ... by the time the Battle of Britain began, pilots of 19 or 20 were typical and even 18 year olds were not uncommon.' (South Cerney.)*

of 1940 into 26 pages, then spread ourselves over May, skipped June and July, and finally settled down for the big bash of August and September. Result: 563 hardback pages.

From start to finish I was never sure what was going to happen to the pilots of my Hornet Squadron until it happened. I knew they would go to France, be bored by the Phoney War, overwhelmed in the Blitzkrieg and outnumbered in the Battle of Britain, but who would live and who would die was something that seemed to emerge, naturally yet unexpectedly, from the flow of the narrative. I didn't so much write the story as record it. For inst-

ance, when Moggy Cattermole arrived I had no idea he was going to develop into such a charming shit. Hart surprised me by showing signs of stuffiness. Flip Moran turned out not to be as tough as he seemed. Skull had a steely streak in him that impressed me. And so on. They became a very individual group, all of them special if not all admirable; and contrary to the myth created by the cinema, the best fighter pilot was not necessarily the most attractive person; sometimes quite the reverse.

In the book there is an exchange between Fanny Barton (then acting CO) and the adjutant, Kellaway (him-

self a former RFC pilot), which I think gets close to the heart of the matter. Fanny, annoyed by some horseplay, wonders why his pilots behave like such bloody lunatics. Kellaway answers:

'Oh well ... They're all a bit mad, you know. They wouldn't do it unless there was a damn good chance of getting killed, would they? They're not what you'd call model citizens, any of them. More like vandals, I suppose. They're just itching to be turned loose with an eight-gun Hurricane on some lumbering great bomber.'

Certainly a fighter pilot's wings created instant sex appeal. The irony is that the appeal should be the product of such a brutal business. All war requires killing; what made the fighter pilot different was that he killed in a spectacular way, and he did it in a uniquely beautiful setting. In 1939 he was one of a few special young men suddenly given hitherto superhuman powers: he could break free of the Earth, climb higher than the Alps, turn, roll, dive, all at astonishing speed; and, above all, by a few seconds' pressure of the thumb he could wipe out another aeroplane just as great and complex and magical as his own; could make it blow itself to pieces and vanish in a brief, bright flowering of flame.

No wonder the fighter pilot found the lure of these powers irresistible. When the war correspondent Alan Moorehead flew with Blenheim pilots fighting the Italians in East Africa in 1940 he wrote:

'Most of them were completely unanalytical. They were restless and nervous when they were grounded for a day ... They lived sharp vivid lives. Their response to almost everything – women, flying, drinking, working – was immediate, positive and direct ... They made friends easily. And never again after the speed and excitement of this war would they lead the lives they were once designed to lead.' (From *African Trilogy* by Alan Moorehead, Hamish Hamilton, 1944.)

And his words hold good for fighter pilots back home.

Off-duty fighter pilots were not all model citizens. Games and stunts in the mess involved debagging, spraying

Above *'Restless and nervous when grounded for a day ...' 'Hart', 'Fitzgerald' and 'Cattermole' wait for the next scramble (Friston).*

Opposite *'They may act like undergraduates, yet their business is war' (Friston).*

24

with fire extinguishers and indoor rugby games. They were young; sometimes it's hard to realise just how young. When war broke out most RAF fighter pilots were in their early twenties at most. By mid-1940 the average had fallen sharply, so much so that pilots of 19 or 20 were typical and even 18-year-olds were not uncommon.

With youth went stamina, resilience and an astonishing spirit of 'press on regardless' which enabled them to fly four or five (or more) sorties a day, day after day. Some who flew in the Battle still insist today that their comrades were 'indefatigable'. However, Group Captain Dennis David (CBE, DFC and Bar), interviewed for a BBC Radio 4 documentary, said his most abiding memory was 'of being very tired'. Wing Commander Bob Doe (DSO, DFC) too, in *Gunbutton to 'Fire'* (William Kimber), remembers 'extreme tiredness'. Not just from the fighting (which was spasmodic) but from the nervous strain of waiting. And the hours were long. 32 Squadron sang a song:

'Our average day is from dawn until
    dusk
Which doesn't sound much I'll
    admit,
But when dawn is at three and dusk
    is at ten,
You'll agree it's a bit of a shit!'

Flight Sergeant (later Squadron Leader) Ginger Lacey (DFM and Bar), flying six or eight times a day, never less than four, week in week out, recalls in *Ginger Lacey – Fighter Pilot* (Robert Hale) that pilots were brought to 'such a state of tiredness that they could not bother even to walk away from their aircraft on landing'; they lay in the shade of the wing and fell instantly asleep. Usually, if they

were scrambled, the adrenalin pumped and the heart thumped, and once in the air again they were okay. Admittedly, fatigue utterly drained a few men to the point where they were flying in a kind of stupor; but in general, youth was the salvation of the young.

One of the things you can do in a novel – and perhaps do best in a novel – is suggest the rare sense of growth and maturing that forms the bonds of comradeship in a fighter squadron. They may act like undergraduates yet their business is war. And although the fighting is important, what matters most is the men. I spent four years on *Piece of Cake*; gave up in despair twice when the story stalled and would not budge; went back to it each time and found that I'd been trying to force it in

the wrong direction. As soon as the characters had been created they knew where they were going, knew a damn sight better than I did. Today, some of those pilots are more alive to me than many of the people I see around me; indeed, they are *doubly* alive since I have got to know the actors who look so eerily like my images of them.

So why did I write *Piece of Cake*? Because I believed it ought to be written, and because nobody else had written it. There have been plenty of novels about RAF fighter pilots but far too many of them have led to a sort of comic-strip image that is grossly unfair to the men of Fighter Command in those days. In *Piece of Cake* I tried to depict them as they really were: human yet special.

TACTICS, SKILLS AND HARDWARE

The lessons learnt in the first year of war

DEREK ROBINSON

Before the Battle of Britain there was the Battle for France, and before the Battle for France there was the Spanish Civil War. That's where the tactics began for the German Air Force. The Luftwaffe used Spain as a testing-ground; and the lessons they learned there made a great difference to their tactics, and therefore to their pilots' chances of survival.

At first the fighter arm of the German air contingent in Spain (the Condor Legion) flew Heinkel 51 biplanes, but when the Republican air force got some good new machines – especially the Russian I-16 Rata, a fast 4-gun monoplane – the Heinkels were outclassed and had to be switched to ground-support tasks. It wasn't until the first Messerschmitt Bf109s arrived that the Condor Legion had a fighter to match the enemy. Even so, two Bf109s were shot down in an early encounter with I-16 Ratas. It was not enough just to have a speedy, powerful aeroplane; you also had to fly it correctly. Initially the German tactics were poor. The Messerschmitts went into battle in close formation, keeping the kind of interlocked pattern that looked impressive but was cramped and clumsy in combat. It didn't take long for the pilots to discover the advantages of spreading out, and this led to the adoption of the 'finger four' formation, so called because it looked like the widespread tips of the fingers, with the middle finger representing the leader and the index finger his wingman, while the other two fingers represent a similar pair alongside.

There was nothing new about this. Both sides had learned in World War One that if a group of aircraft opened out and created plenty of elbow-room they could protect one another, search the sky, and manoeuvre without constantly having to worry about collision. They then forgot it all. The Luftwaffe re-employed this tactic in Spain. Werner Mölders – one of several German fighter pilots who honed their skills in Spain – contributed much to this thinking. The Condor Legion went back to basics. It established the pair (or *Rotte*) as the smallest, most efficient unit. It consisted of a leader and his wingman, flying about 200 yards apart. Ideally, the wingman was up-sun of his leader but behind and slightly below him, where he could protect his tail, while the leader could similarly guard his wingman without looking up into the dazzle. Two pairs made a *Schwärme*, with the second pair

'If there is any beauty in war, it must lie in the aircraft.' Mark Hanna flies over Charlton Park.

angled back from the first and maintaining different heights. In this way the *Schwärme* covered itself from nearly all angles of attack; and since the four aircraft were scattered over more than a quarter of a mile of sky, the formation was far less conspicuous than the thick clumps of planes favoured by the Republicans, or the Italians – who suffered much heavier losses in Spain than the Condor Legion.

The RAF did not totally ignore the German experiments in Spain. When the civil war was over, an Air Staff officer visited Spanish Republican aircrew being held in a refugee camp near Perpignan, in France. They told him three things. First, the standard of German flying in Spain had been very high; second, the damage from the 'explosive bullets' of the cannon-armed Me 109s had caused a severe drop in Republican pilots' morale; and third, to counter this, the thickness of the armour plating at each Republican pilot's back was increased to 7 mm, and 'the pilots were unanimous that this protection had saved many lives'. The officer submitted his report to the Air Fighting Committee at the Air Ministry on 5 July 1939. (Source: Public Records Office.)

Before the war broke out, the RAF thought that aerial warfare would involve fighters attacking bombers, more specifically, formations of the one attacking formations of the other. Bombers would take off from bases in Germany and cross the North Sea – too far for fighter escorts – and RAF fighters would engage them, using the appropriate Fighting Area Attack, of which there were six. These were highly choreographed procedures, and they had to be performed just so – 'like guardsmen on parade', is how Wing

The Luftwaffe fighter patrolled in pairs with the leader covered from behind by his wingman. Nick Grace in Me 109 pursued by Mark Hanna in Spitfire, with Reg Hallam in Me 109 chasing his tail (Friston).

Commander Tom Neil recalled them in *Gunbutton to 'Fire'*.

Here is a sample of No. 2 Attack.

At first, two sections of three fighters formate, so that one is behind the other. The No. 1 section leader manoeuvres to approach the enemy from astern and he transmits warning orders for attack. Then in the words of the RAF's contemporary Manual of Air Tactics:

'The section leader selects as his target the outside aircraft on one flank of the enemy formation. At a suitable distance away from the enemy he orders echelon port or starboard. Numbers 2 and 3 of the section form echelon at 45 degrees.

'When steady and about 400 yards away from the enemy, the section leader gives the executive order for the attack. R/T order by formation leader, "No. 2 Attack, No. 2 Attack – Go."

'Thereupon Nos. 2 and 3 pick up their respective targets in accordance with their positions in the formation. Each fighter aircraft maintains this approximate formation and fires as soon as he comes to optimum range.

'When the leader of the section decides to break away, he will do so to the opposite side to that on which his section is echeloned. Nos. 2 and 3 follow in quick succession by the shortest route, keeping their next ahead in view. They will then re-form on the leader.'

No. 2 section now repeats the whole procedure.

The problem with a Fighting Area Attack was that it demanded continuous tight-formation flying by the fighters. Witness the experience of Pilot Officer (now Wing Commander) Roland Beamont (DSO and Bar, OBE, DFC and Bar) on 10 May 1940. He was part of a three-squadron formation patrolling Valenciennes at 10,000 feet. 'We made a fine sight as 36 Hurricanes formed up ... in three squadron boxes, line-astern, four sections of Vic-Threes to a squadron ... And then without fuss or drama, about ten Messerschmitt 109s appeared ... out of some high cloud.' The big wing turned towards them. The 109s, free from the restrictions of close formation, 'dived one after the other on to the tail sections of the Wing'. They shot down four Hurricanes. (From *Fighter Command* by Chaz Bowyer, Dent 1980.)

As the Battle of Britain went on, some squadrons almost instinctively loosened their formations and fought in pairs, not threes; nevertheless, Fighting Area Attacks remained official policy.

As the war progressed, however, the RAF learnt by experience and made changes to its tactics and to its machines.

When war had broken out, machine guns in Fighter Command were harmonised at 400 yards, meaning that the eight guns on a Hurricane or Spitfire were focused so that their bullet streams converged to form an 'area of lethal density' at a range of 400 yards. It was known as the Dowding Spread, named after Air Chief Marshal Dowding, Commander-in-Chief of Fighter Command.

As Air Vice-Marshal Johnny Johnson (CBE, DSO, DFC) has explained, the Dowding Spread helped the average fighter pilot because it gave him a fairly large 'shot-gun' bullet pattern at long range. But it didn't help the good shots who liked to close to a range of 250 yards or less before firing. By April 1940 the sporadic scraps over France had taught Hurricane pilots to abandon the Dowding Spread and reharmonise to 250 yards, and eventually each squadron was allowed to harmonise as it thought best.

Pilots had also been ordered to fire in one long continuous burst and not several short bursts, each of which, it was said, depressed the nose and took the sights off the target. Combat soon taught the pilots otherwise: brief bursts were best. Similarly, the recommended method of attack for a single fighter was to approach the enemy at full

'Fanny' Barton (Tom Burlinson).

speed. Flight Sergeant Ginger Lacey did this over France in May 1940 and swept right past the enemy before he could open fire.

When No. 1 Squadron – based in eastern France during the Phoney War – discovered that a German pilot had thick armour-plating behind him, they began fitting it to their own aircraft and back armour subsequently became standard. As a result, all RAF fighter pilots flew with greater confidence. For instance, when Pilot Officer Wally Wallens (now Squadron Leader, DFC) was attacked from behind, one bullet hit his left sleeve and knocked the face off his wrist-watch while another smashed his right earphone; but his back-armour stopped several cannon shells. However, one shell hit his leg:

Piece of Cake's Spitfires in tight echelon starboard. Close formation obliges pilots to keep a constant eye on the next aircraft.

back-armour was not yet full-length.

So at the start of the Battle of Britain there can be little doubt that tactically the Luftwaffe had the advantage. Spain had paid off. There were other differences, too, in hardware. Unlike the Me 109, the Spitfire did not have the advantage of fuel-injection and if its pilot shoved the nose hard down, his engine cut out for a few seconds; to avoid this, he had to half-roll into the dive. On the other hand, a prolonged dive made the 109's controls very stiff indeed, and its latticed canopy gave a view inferior to that of the RAF fighters. At height, the Spitfire and the 109 were very comparable. Below 15,000 feet the Hurricane had some important advantages. Its thick wing made a rock-solid gun platform, with four guns closely grouped together in each wing. The 109 was too small and light to carry eight guns. The Hurricane was so big and robust it could absorb terrible punishment and still get home. Its rugged, widespread under-carriage was much more user-friendly than the 109's narrow legs, which certainly contributed to the great number of ground-loops the Luftwaffe suffered in landing accidents.

Fighter Command's communications improved when some squadrons got VHF radios, far better than the old HF equipment with its range of only 30 or 40 miles; and marksmanship was helped by the introduction of de Wilde incendiary ammunition, which sparkled on impact and showed the pilot he was on target.

RAF squadrons improved their tactics in 1940, often by adding a couple of 'weavers' behind the formation to weave about and watch for trouble. The position was known as 'Arse-End Charlie' and it was not popular; too many weavers vanished. Another de-

'Flip' Moran (Gerard O'Hare).

Opposite *The German advance in the spring of 1940 brought an abrupt end to the Phoney War. Tim Woodward 'Squadron Leader Rex', scrambles as 'St Pierre' is strafed (Charlton Park).*

vice was the 'snake', in which the entire formation, in line-astern, weaved like a snake. This was wearying, expensive in fuel, and not noticeably safer.

Meanwhile the Luftwaffe had made three great blunders: they ignored Britain's radar, they failed to give their 109s drop-tanks, and as the Battle wore on they increasingly shackled their fighters to their bombers. It is very hard to fathom why the Germans did not try to destroy Britain's radar defences.

By February 1940, 29 radar stations were distributed around the British coastline, from the Bristol Channel to

Above 'Fatigue drained a few men to the point where they were flying in a kind of stupor; but in general youth was the salvation of the young.'

Opposite German experience in the Spanish Civil War gave the Luftwaffe an early advantage.

the Orkneys, with more being added. The transmitter aerial masts were 350 feet high, the receivers 250 feet high. Any determined series of raids on them could have knocked great holes in the radar chain. In fact, the Luftwaffe hit the chain hard only once. On 12 August 1940 they attacked five radar stations, from Ventnor in the Isle of Wight to Dover, knocked out four, and immediately sent in fresh raids through the gaps to bomb RAF fighter fields. Briefly, a large part of Fighter Command's defences was blind.

Fighter Command was heavily out-numbered at the start of the Battle. 591 RAF fighters faced about 1,200 bombers, 280 dive-bombers, 220 twin-engine fighters and 760 single-engine fighters. Radar made every RAF fighter worth three or four, and thus went a long way towards restoring the balance. For a start, radar made it unnecessary to mount standing patrols (except at first over convoys). Squadrons were spared the strain of constantly keeping aircraft in the sky *in case* the enemy attacked; and when the raiders came, the RAF fighters were usually up and waiting for them. It was

Above To discourage carelessness fines were imposed on pilots who damaged their Spitfires. (Squadron Leader Ramsey runs his Spitfire into a slit trench).

not good for German morale – no matter how they changed their route, height or timing, they would always meet Spitfires or Hurricanes.

Radar was not perfect in 1940. It was pretty accurate as regards range and bearing, less so on height, and downright unreliable on strength. So a radar station could report confidently that it had a plot (say) 30 miles away flying (say) north-west, but had more difficulty in deciding how many planes it involved, and at what height. What's

more, the enemy became adept at sending up spoof raids, which never went anywhere, and decoy raids, which went somewhere but only for the purpose of drawing off the defence from the real raid, which might itself divide into two groups with targets far apart. And these were only a few of the problems faced by Fighter Command's controllers. If they scrambled a squadron too soon, it would run low on fuel before the real threat matured; if too late, it would still be struggling for

Spitfires at Charlton Park, the Wiltshire estate which was used to represent Château St Pierre, The Piece of Cake *squadron's base in eastern France. The 17th-century house with its grass runway was an ideal location. To make it suitable for Spitfires, the airstrip was widened and extended, though when shooting began in February they had to make do with just 600 yards of muddy grass.*

Right *Aerial cameraman Simon Werry gets an Me109 in his sights from the back of the B25 camera ship, while* below *Mark Hanna enjoys the scenery at Charlton Park.*

Top *Me 109 chases MkI Spitfire over Sussex.*
Above *Spitfire MkIX, MH434.*
Left *Vic formation with 'tail end Charlie'.*

Overleaf *Vortices from the Spitfire's propellor swirl the smoke of a hundred burning tyres at Charlton Park.*

Anticlockwise from top
Replica Spitfire and period vehicles at 'St Pierre'.

Special effects enliven the celebrations at Wrotham Park.

Spitfire at Duxford.

Cambridge airport stood in for Le Touquet: the aircraft is a de Havilland Rapide.

Hornet Squadron over Wiltshire.

As they gained experience from combat, RAF pilots often flew in loose pairs, like the Luftwaffe's fighters, rather than tight formations. These photographs taken from the B25 camera ship show how formation flying calls for the pilot to keep a constant eye on the next aircraft, leaving the leader to scan the hostile sky.

Opposite *End of sports. Spitfire replica on its nose at South Cerney.*

Left *A MkXI Spitfire (with retracted tailwheel) and a MkIX over Oxford.*

Below *Reg Hallam (black nose) and Walther Eichorn (red nose) over Duxford. The Messerschmitts in* Piece of Cake *were built in Spain after the war and equipped with British Merlin engines.*

height when the raiders arrived.

Height was crucial. Every fighter pilot hated to be caught below the enemy. Because radar-predicted heights were unreliable, controllers sometimes added a couple of thousand feet on the principle that it was better to send the fighters too high than too low; and a fighter leader who had recently been bounced might add another thousand or two for the same reason. But this, of course, might put the fighters a mile or so above the raid, which could therefore just slip past them, especially as the Germans listened carefully to RAF controllers' instructions and sometimes altered height accordingly. To counter this, Fighter Command changed its code-word so that, for instance, 'Angels eight' meant not 8,000 feet but 10,000 feet and so on. It was an endless guessing game.

Radar only faced out to sea. Over land, a network of Observer Corps posts reported to Fighter Command – but cloud or haze might obscure their view. Sometimes a cluster of bombers flew across England without being intercepted.

Given that the Luftwaffe knew Fighter Command was waiting for its Heinkel 111s, Junkers 88s and Dornier 17s, the German fighters were always going to be busy. Without drop-tanks the Me 109 had an endurance of about 90 minutes, which meant it could just about reach the outskirts of London if it turned round and went straight home. Messerschmitt pilots never had enough time to fight. When escorting bombers, they never had more than 20 minutes in which to engage the RAF fighters; after that, a glance at the fuel gauge and simple arithmetic told them to beat it. With a stretch of water to cross, perhaps being harried by the enemy yet unable to risk a scrap for fear of running out of fuel – this is not a happy experience for a pilot.

Why the Luftwaffe never fitted drop-tanks on the 109 in 1940 is yet another mystery. It wouldn't have been difficult (the Japanese already had drop-tanks on their Zero fighters) and it would have given the 109 an extra 30 minutes in the combat area. The margin of the Battle was narrow enough as it was. Not having drop-tanks was an act of crass generosity to Fighter Command on the part of the Luftwaffe.

This was all the more so when the German bomber pilots began to demand close escort by their fighters. In the first half of the Battle the Luftwaffe used its fighters intelligently – that is, as fighters, free to exploit their speed and performance. As a rule they either flew high escort, where they could use the advantage height gave them, or they flew freebooting missions to distract and destroy the enemy. German fighter pilots hated the idea of close escort. Shackling them to the bombers deprived them of height, speed and freedom of manoeuvre. It abused the design of the fighter, whose function is to fight, not to hold hands with bombers. Tactically, the Luftwaffe deployed its fighters with more emotion than logic as the Battle wore on; and, as soon became evident, the Germans paid for it.

While they made the mistake of neglecting Britain's radar installations, the Luftwaffe hit repeatedly at South coast airfields in the summer of 1940. (Another replica Spitfire goes up at Friston.)

FIGHTING MACHINES
The aircraft they fought in

M~IKE~ J~ERRAM~

The prototype of perhaps the most famous aircraft in history, less charismatically known as the F37/34 or Type 300, first flew early in the morning of 5 March 1936 from Eastleigh, near Southampton, piloted by the Vickers' company's chief test pilot 'Mutt' Summers. Despite the patchy appearance of its unpainted metal panels, the hand-built prototype was an uncommonly handsome machine with flowing lines which ran virtually unbroken from its close-cowled 1,025 hp Rolls Royce Merlin C engine to its tail, and a thin wing of perfect elliptical planform.

Within three months the Air Ministry placed an order for 310 of these Spitfires, although Mitchell, creator of the Schneider Trophy-winning Supermarine S6 seaplanes, was never to see them fly. Even as his prototype took off that spring morning, he was dying of a stomach cancer which successive bouts of surgery had failed to arrest. He carried on with production design work until his death at the age of 42 years on 11 June 1937, after handing over his final masterpiece to Supermarine's

'An uncommonly handsome machine'–Mark Hanna taking off in the Old Flying Machine Company's MkIX Spitfire at Friston.

chief draughtsman, Joe Smith.

By that time production of the aeroplane had begun at Supermarine's small factory at Woolston on Southampton Water. Supermarine had never before built more than 25 aircraft to any one contract, but was now faced with meeting an increased order for 510 aircraft in a factory ill-equipped to handle high-volume production. So only the aircraft's fuselages were manufactured at Woolston; all other components were supplied by subcontractors. It soon became apparent that even their combined efforts would not meet demand. A 'shadow' factory was planned at Castle Bromwich near Birmingham, and a further contract for 1,000 aircraft placed before work had even begun on the new plant.

The first production Spitfire Mark I flew from Eastleigh on 14 May 1938. The first RAF squadrons to receive the aircraft were Nos. 19 and 66, both based at RAF Duxford in Cambridgeshire where, appropriately, some of the aerial scenes for *Piece of Cake* were shot. Initial deliveries were dismally slow with just one new Spitfire appearing each week, for unlike the Hawker Hurricane, the Spitfire, with stressed-skin monocoque airframe, complex curvature and subtlety of line, was not best fitted to mass production techniques. It has been calculated that

'Like a beautiful bird feeling its way to the roost' – Doug Arnold's MkIX Spitfire NH238 lands at Friston.

it took 330,000 man-hours – the equivalent of three whole working lifetimes – to build one machine. When war was declared only nine RAF fighter squadrons had Spitfires.

The first Spitfire Mark Is were similar to the prototype, but early service experience soon brought improvements which included a castoring tailwheel instead of a skid, and a 1,030 hp Merlin II engine driving a three-blade two-speed propeller instead of a fixed-pitch airscrew which increased maximum speed by five miles per hour. Armoured glass windscreens were fitted at the insistence of RAF Fighter Command's Commander-in-Chief Dowding, who pointed out not unreasonably that if Al Capone's Chicago gangsters could ride in bullet-proof limousines he saw no reason why his pilots should not enjoy the same protection in their aeroplanes. Armour plate behind the pilot was also soon adopted: from the rear came the greatest danger of sudden death. Standard 'A' wing Spitfire Mark I armament consisted of eight 0.303 Colt Browning Mk II machine guns, each with 300 rounds of ammunition. The Mark IIA, which entered service in the latter stages of the Battle of Britain, had improved Browning IIs with higher rates of fire, while 'B' wing variants had a 20 mm Hispano cannon in place of the inboard pair of machine guns on each wing.

Spitfires first saw combat on 16 October 1939 when aircraft from No. 603 (City of Edinburgh) Squadron shot down a Luftwaffe Heinkel He 111 in the Firth of Forth. A fortnight later Flying Officer Archibald M'Kellar of No. 602 (City of Glasgow) Squadron brought down another Heinkel on the Lammermuir Hills near Dalkeith – the first enemy aircraft actually to crash on British soil. A contemporary report noted: 'The German rear gunner, who had been fighting back, was suddenly silent … The big 'plane shuddered, lost height, climbed again to clear the roof of a farmhouse, and then slid on its belly up a sloping field. Once, almost as if it were trying to make the air again, the Heinkel soared, only to fall back mortally wounded. M'Kellar, triumphant, circled overhead.' (From *Glasgow's Fighter Squadron* by F. G. Nancarrow, 1942.)

One of the few remaining early Spitfires with a distinguished combat history. MH434 was one of the aircraft which took part in filming The Battle of Britain *20 years ago.*

Doug Arnold's MkXI Spitfire PL983 (near camera) with MkIX MH434 over Wiltshire.

When the Battle of Britain started in July 1940, RAF Fighter Command had 19 squadrons of Spitfires, eight of them based with 11 Group in southern England. Production was running at five per day, still less than half the rate achieved by Hawker for the easier-to-build Hurricane. But it was the shortage of experienced pilots, not aeroplanes, which posed the greatest problem. Many of the pilots were mere tyros to whom the Spitfire must have seemed very daunting after the Tiger Moths and Miles Magisters in which they had trained. With nearly ten times the power, a slippery airframe, sharp-reflexed controls and an as yet unfamiliar retractable undercarriage, they were still vulnerable to accidents. To discourage carelessness, fines were imposed on pilots who damaged their Spitfires: five shillings for taxiing with flaps lowered, where propeller-blown debris could damage them, or with the

cockpit door left unlatched to bang against the fuselage skinning, or for boiling the Merlin engine's coolant through prolonged taxiing; five *pounds* if they landed with the undercarriage up or were too heavy on the brakes and tipped a Spitfire on to its nose. Ladders and lengths of rope with which to recover the upended Spitfires of heavy-handed pilots were tools of the trade for RAF crash crews. The money went to the ground crews who had to repair the aircraft, and who grew modestly rich as pilots grew careful in ground handling the Spitfire on its narrow track undercarriage.

But in the air the 'Spit', although far from perfect, excelled in the hands of a skilled pilot able to exploit its well harmonised controls. Experienced Spitfire fliers contend that Supermarine never did quite get the fighter's pitch control sorted out, even in the final production models.

The Spitfire IA, which was the principal version used up to the Battle of Britain, was – on paper at least – marginally faster than the Messerschmitt Me 109E in level flight, though the German fighter could climb faster below 20,000 feet, after which the Spitfire's lower wing loading gave it the edge in manoeuvrability, except at low airspeed.

The first year of war was only the prologue to the Spitfire's protracted career. Total production ran to more

Three MkIX's and a MkI turn to camera: MH434 (in the foreground) NM238, AR213 and ML417 in formation near Duxford, where much of Piece of Cake's *aerial filming was done.*

than 22,500 aircraft in two dozen major marks. Few names are so evocative, nor any aircraft held in such enduring affection not just by those who flew them, but even by young children born to the supersonic travel of the 1980s whose grandparents only dimly remember those tense summer months of 1940.

Some 160 Spitfires are thought to be in existence around the world, although only a few are still flying. No contemporary 1939 Spitfire Mark Is are flying. Those which took part in *Piece of Cake* are later variants, painted as they would have been at the time of the action. They are as follows.

AR213/G-AIST. Spitfire Mark IA, the second oldest Spitfire still flying. Built by Westland Aircraft at Yeovil in the summer of 1941, it saw no combat but was allocated to No. 57 Operational Training Unit at Hawarden, near Chester, and served in the operational training role until put into storage in August 1944. AR213 was sold in March 1947 to the late Air Commodore Allen Wheeler (who also bought Spitfire Mark V AB910, now part of The Battle of Britain Memorial Flight) and was stored at Old Warden Aerodrome with the Shuttleworth Trust Collection, of which the Air Commodore was a Trustee. Refurbished to fly for filming *The Battle of Britain* in 1967-8, AR213 was later sold to the late Hon. Patrick Lindsay, international director of Christie's, who regularly flew it from its base at Wycombe Air

The large squadron identification letters were the bane of everyone's life. They peeled off in mid-air, taking paint with them and were a trial for director, art department and continuity supervisor. We decided to drop them after the first episode.

Park, Buckinghamshire. A classic eight-gun Spitfire, AR213, is still owned by the Lindsay family and maintained by Personal Plane Services.

MH434/G-ASJV. Cannon-armed Spitfire LF IXB, built in August 1943 at Vickers-Armstrong's Castle Bromwich factory. While being flown by Flight Lieutenant H.P. Lardner-Burke, DFC, of 222 (Natal) Squadron at RAF Hornchurch, Essex on 'Ramrod' daylight bomber escort missions during late August and early September 1943, MH434 was credited with shooting down two Focke Wulf Fw 190s, damaging a third, and was awarded a 'shared-kill' of a Messerschmitt Me 109F. Sold after the war to the Netherlands Air Force, it flew 165 sorties against the Nationalist forces in Indonesia before being sold again to the Belgian Air Force and subsequently to Belgian civil target-towing contractor COGEA. In June 1963 MH434 returned to England under private ownership and joined the large fleet of Spitfires gathered for filming *The Battle of Britain* during 1968. Subsequently bought by Sir Adrian Swire, it became a familiar sight at airshows, flown exuberantly by the late Neil Williams and by former Red Arrows leader Ray Hanna, who, on behalf of a consortium of buyers, made a successful (and then record) bid of £260,000 for it at Christie's auction in April 1983. Since then MH434 has been based with Ray's Old Flying Machine Company collection of warbirds at Duxford Airfield, Cambridgeshire, and usually wears the colours and ZD-B code letters of No. 222 (Natal) Squadron.

ML417/G-BJSG. Cannon-armed Spitfire LF IXE, built at Castle Bromwich in early 1944. It served with No. 443 (Royal Canadian Air Force) Squadron at Ford, Sussex, operating from a forward base at St Croix Sur-Mer after D-Day. Two Focke Wulf Fw 190s were claimed as 'probables' and two Messerschmitt Me 109s as confirmed 'kills' during this period. In 1948 ML417 was converted into a two-seat Spitfire T9 trainer for export to the Indian Air Force. Its airframe was discovered in a storage compound of the IAF Museum at Palam in 1967 and shipped to the United States three years later. British warbird collector Stephen Grey brought ML417 to England in 1982 and a major restoration, rebuild and reconversion to single-seat standard was undertaken at Wycombe Air Park, where the aircraft took to the air again on 10 February 1984. Now based with The Fighter Collection at Duxford Airfield, and usually seen with clipped wingtips of the LF IXE variant and wearing the 2I-T code and D-Day invasion stripes it carried with No. 443 Squadron, 2nd Tactical Air Force, ML417 was fitted with elliptical wingtips for *Piece of Cake*.

NH238/G-MKIX. Spitfire LF IXC/E, built at Castle Bromwich in the spring of 1944. Flown for only 122 hours in RAF service with No. 84 Group Support Unit in Hampshire, it was sold to the Royal Netherlands Air Force in 1947, serving in anti-guerilla operations in Indonesia before returning to Holland as an advanced trainer. Like MH434, it ended up with COGEA in Belgium, and came back to England in May 1961 as the mount of well-known racing pilot Beverley Snook. After suffering damage while taking part that year in the London-

Max boost – Stephen Grey takes ML417 off in characteristically energetic style at Charlton Park.

Cardiff Air race, the Spitfire was sold to a private museum maintained by the manufacturers of 'Queen Mary' low-loader trailers. In 1970 NH238 journeyed to the United States, where it was restored to flying condition for a member of the Confederate Air Force. Now owned by noted Spitfire collector (and wartime Spitfire pilot) Douglas Arnold, whose D-A personal code it normally carries, it flew again in Britain for the first time on 6 May 1984.

PL983/G-PRXI. Spitfire PR XI photographic reconnaissance aircraft, one of 417 of that variant built. It was manufactured at Reading in October 1944 and operated by No. 34 Wing, 2nd Tactical Air Force at Blackbushe, and Nos. 2 and 4 Squadrons in Holland during the latter stages of the war. On 27 January 1948 the Spitfire was handed over at RAF Hendon to Tony Satterthwaite, United States Air Attaché to Britain, as his personal transport and was raced on several occasions that year by former Air Transport Auxiliary pilot Lettice Curtis, who set a British Women's closed circuit speed record of 312.208 mph in it. When Mr Satterthwaite returned to the USA the Spitfire was stored and then donated to the Shuttleworth Trust Collection at Old Warden Aerodrome, Bedfordshire, in 1950. There it remained until 1975 when PL983 was moved to Duxford Airfield for the start of a complete restoration, which was proceeding well when the Trust elected to sell the aircraft at auction in April 1983. Its new owner was Frenchman Roland Fraissinet, a former Spitfire pilot, who commissioned Trent Aero at East Midlands Airport to complete the restoration. PL983/G-PRXI flew again for the first time in 34 years on 18 July 1984, and holds the dinstinction – albeit tempor-

ary – of being the world's most expensive Spitfire. Present owner Douglas Arnold paid £300,000 for it at Christie's auction at Bournemouth Airport in October 1987.

MK297/N9BL, a Mark IX Spitfire, owned by the Confederate Air Force, also makes a brief appearance in *Piece*

Above *'Flash' Gordon (Nathaniel Parker).*

Opposite *Hart (Boyd Gaines).*

of Cake, attacking the CAF's Heinkel bomber. Also featured in *The Battle of Britain*, the aircraft flew for many years without cannon, which were restored for the filming of *Piece of Cake* so that it would resemble Ray Hanna's Spitfire.

Hurricane

In 1933 Hawker Aircraft's chief designer Sydney Camm presented plans to the Air Ministry for a high speed monoplane development of the Hawker Fury biplane which was then the RAF's front-line fighter. The bureaucrats were sceptical that an aeroplane could be made to fly at 280 mph, or that pilots would be able to handle it if it did.

Undaunted, Camm, backed by the Hawker Board, continued with his design, and within a year came a ministerial change of heart. 300 mph fighters now looked a distinct possibility with the development of Rolls-Royce's new 1,000 hp PV-12 aero engine. Camm swiftly redesigned his proposed Fury Monoplane around the new power plant, but with four guns instead of the eight demanded by the Air Ministry, whose scientists had concluded that a minimum of 250 strikes by rifle-calibre ammunition would be needed to bring down an enemy bomber. Since an average pilot could not be expected to keep a target in his sights for more than two seconds, and 1,000 rounds per minute was the fire rate of each gun, eight guns would be needed to deliver a death blow.

Hawker was awarded a contract for a prototype F 36/34, which first flew on 6 November 1935 in the hands of chief test pilot P.W.S. 'George' Bulman. 'It's a piece of cake, I could even teach you to fly her in half an hour,' he told the non-pilot Camm after the maiden

flight. Camm was less sanguine, and later admitted that he had doubts about the aircraft. Given more time, he believed he could have designed a thinner, more efficient wing which would have made his fighter the greatest of its day.

Hawker's chairman, Sir Thomas Sopwith, who celebrated his centenary in 1988, had no such qualms. He ordered materials, stocks and bought-in components for an unprecedented 1,000 aircraft production run even before the RAF had conducted flight trials. His gamble paid off. In the summer of 1936 the Air Ministry ordered 600 aircraft, the largest order which had ever been placed in peacetime for a British aircraft.

At Camm's suggestion the new fighter was named 'Hurricane'. The first service aircraft, now armed with the requisite eight 0.303 Browning machine guns, was delivered to 111 Squadron at RAF Northolt near London on 17 December 1937 and within two months all 16 of the squadron's aircraft were operational, although the novelties of high landing speed, retractable undercarriage and a fully enclosed cockpit took their toll in landing accidents in the transition to the new aircraft. On 10 February 1938 the squadron's commanding officer, Squadron Leader John Gillan, made a morale-boosting flight from his base to Edinburgh and back, riding a Hurricane in both senses on the return trip when a ferocious tailwind increased his average groundspeed to 456 mph – nearly 150 mph faster than the Hurricane's officially acknowledged maximum speed. Secrecy surrounding the fighter's true capability permitted only the revelation that he had managed 408 mph. Officialdom saw no need to mention the obliging tailwind, although Treble One's CO was thereafter known as 'Downwind' Gillan!

At the time of the Munich crisis in 1938, production had built up to eight per week, so that by the outbreak of war 18 squadrons of Hurricane Is were operational with Fighter Command. Four were immediately despatched to support the British Expeditionary Force. The aircraft's first combat victory came on 30 October 1939 when Pilot Officer P.W.O. Mould of No. 1 Squadron shot down one of three Dornier Do 17 bombers attacking the airfield at Vassincourt.

Throughout the winter of 1939/40

the rugged Hurricane was able to continue flying from rutted airfields unusable by other types. Ten squadrons eventually went to France, covering battlefields and providing escorts for RAF daylight bombing raids while fighting desperately against uneven odds which saw more than 200 Hurricanes lost in ten days before the Dunkirk evacuation, many destroyed on the ground or abandoned in hasty retreat from makeshift airfields.

Production, meanwhile, was in full flow from two Hawker factories and from the Gloster Aircraft Company, which jointly produced 1,373 aircraft in the first eight months of 1940. At the outbreak of the Battle of Britain 29 RAF squadrons were equipped with Hurricanes and 19 with Spitfires. The burden of defence was to fall principally on the Hawker fighter, 1,715 Hurricanes taking part in the Battle – more than all other fighter types taken together. The Hurricane was a match for German Messerschmitt Me 109Es only at medium altitude, so it was assigned the less glamorous but more important role of attacking Luftwaffe bomber formations. Ironically, while the name of the Spitfire remains synonymous with the Battle of Britain, the Hurricane played a far more important part, accounting for the destruction of more enemy aircraft than all other defences combined, including anti-aircraft fire.

The Hurricane was quite different in concept to the Spitfire. Bigger, sturdier and slower – by about 40 mph for equivalent early Marks – with a maximum speed of 324 mph at 16,000 feet, its maximum operating altitude was theoretically 30,000 feet, but above 20,000 feet the Hurricane I's performance was anything but sparkling, as this squadron ditty acknowledged:

Above *Fitzgerald (Jeremy Northam).*

Opposite *Pilot Maker MkI – Tiger Moth in early World War Two markings at South Cerney.*

'You'll never get to heaven in a
Hurricane One,
You'll stall before your journey's
done,
Oh, you'll never get to heaven in a
Hurri One,
You'll stall before your journey's
done,
I ain't gonna grieve my lord no
more!'

But the Hurricane possessed qualities which more than compensated. Its outmoded airframe of welded steel tube, wooden formers and stringers, and fabric covering (even on the wings of early Mark Is) may have lacked the aesthetic appeal of the Spitfire's monocoque, but it was strong, quicker and cheaper to build, and easy to repair, familiar to any fitter or rigger who had

worked on Hawker's between-wars biplanes. While a damaged Spitfire might have to be dismantled and returned to the factory or to one of Lord Beaverbrook's Civilian Repair Organisations, a Hurricane could often be patched up *in situ* at squadron level, and when more extensive repair was needed, return to service was swift. A CRO once replaced both wings and all eight machine guns on a Hurricane in just under two hours, and could undertake a complete rebuild in two days.

Pilots loved the 'Hurribox'. It was more forgiving than a Spitfire, a superbly stable gun platform. Its humpbacked cockpit was roomier, more comfortable and afforded better vision. The rugged airframe could absorb extraordinary punishment without catastrophic failure, and the wide-track undercarriage made it easier to land, especially for an injured or combat-exhausted pilot, and was more suited to the rough grass airfields and bomb-damaged tarmac which was its usual environment in 1939/40.

The Hurricane was never extensively developed, but it was employed in all imaginable (and a few unimaginable) roles in a service career which spanned every year and theatre of the war.

Tiger Moth

Tiger Moths only appear fleetingly in *Piece of Cake*, but they played an important part in training many, if not most of the pilots who flew early in the war.

First flown in 1931, the Tiger Moth was no product of inspired genius or meticulous planning, but a hastily cobbled together prototype based on the successful DH 60 Moth lightplane which unexpectedly emerged as one of the legendary training aeroplanes.

Trickier to fly than the contemporary Avro Tutor, intolerant of sloppy handling and apt to magnify – though never to the point of danger – any shortcoming in technique, the 'Tiggie' was popular with instructors and the bane of students' lives. It was said that if you could fly a Tiger Moth well you would be able to fly *anything*.

Tigers had teeth, too. In the desperate days of 1940 (when Nazi invasion looked imminent) provision was made for fitting bomb racks to carry eight 25 lb bombs beneath a Tiger Moth. More bizarre was a device called Paraslasher, invented at the Reid & Sigrist Flying School at Desford, Leicestershire. It comprised a scythe attached to an eight-foot-long pole which could be swung down through the Tiger Moth's floor, and was intended to cut the parachute shroud lines of invading Wehrmacht paratroopers as Tiger Moths flew among them. A flying instructor at Desford demonstrated the technique with great gusto on straw effigies of Hitler and Mussolini.

The precise number of Tiger Moths built is the subject of endless dispute, 8,389 being a commonly accepted figure. A substantial number, perhaps 700 or more, survive, many in flying condition. In the 1950s they were disposed of for as little as £50 each. Today a pristine restored Tiger will fetch about £25,000. Those appearing in *Piece of Cake* are G-ARAZ owned by former RAF pilot Colin Dodds, leader of the de Havilland Moth Club's Tiger Moth Diamond Nine formation display team, and two operated by the Cambridge Flying Group at Cambridge Airport, with whom you may still learn to fly in open cockpit, leather helmet and goggles, just as RAF pilots did half a century ago.

Dragon Rapide

First flown on 17 April 1934, the de Havilland DH 89 Dragon Rapide

Few pilots lived to remember this image in their rear view mirror. Nick Grace's shark-like Hispano Messerschmitt flashes past the tail of the Harvard which was adapted to be one of Piece of Cake's fleet of camera ships.

(originally called Dragon Six) was designed as a six-passenger airliner, powered by two 200 hp DH Gipsy Queen engines. When war was declared on 3 September 1939, all civil flying came under the control of the National Air Communications organisation and many Rapides were impressed into service with No. 24 Squadron, RAF, for use as courier aircraft between Britain and the British Expeditionary Force in France. Ten Rapides were lost in the evacuation. During World War Two 523 examples of the military Dominie version were built, most by the Brush Coachworks company at Loughborough, Leicestershire. Dominies were used as communications aircraft and as navigation and wireless telegraphy trainers. In peacetime many Dominies were converted for civil use, forming the nucleus of numerous small airlines and charter companies in the post-war years. Several continued operating passenger services in Britain into the 1970s.

About 40 of the 722 Rapides and Dominies built between 1934 and 1946 are known to survive. G-AHGD, the Dominie seen in *Piece of Cake*, is kept in immaculate airworthy condition by owner Michael Astor. It wears the authentic camouflage and markings of one of two ex-civil Rapides handed over to the RAF at Hendon on 21 May 1941 by Lady Maud Carnegie. The Rapides had been subscribed for by the Silver Thimble Fund and spent the war years serving as air ambulances in Scotland. Michael Astor's Rapide is painted as *Women of the Empire*. The other Silver Thimble Fund aircraft was named *Women of Britain*.

Two other Rapides make brief appearances in *Piece of Cake*. G-ACZE, owned by Brian Woodford, and G-

AJHO, owned by Colin Dodds, both in crimson and blue paintwork, represent civil airliners of the late Thirties.

Messerschmitt Me 109

It is one of those supreme ironies of fate that Germany's best known fighter should have started and ended its career powered by a British Rolls-Royce engine.

Grudgingly invited by Minister of Aviation Erhard Milch to compete with the Arado, Focke-Wulf and Heinkel companies for a contract to build a new fighter aircraft for the Luftwaffe, Professor Willi Messerschmitt began work on an ambitious concept making use of the most advanced techniques known in the mid-1930s: all-metal monocoque airframe, low cantilever wings, retractable undercarriage, fully enclosed cockpit and the most powerful aero engine then available in Germany, a 610 hp liquid-cooled V-12 Junkers Jumo 210A. But since the Jumo was not ready by the time Messerschmitt had completed his prototype Me 109VI, he substituted a Rolls-Royce Kestrel, forerunner of the Merlin which was to power the Spitfires and Hurricanes against which the German fighter would soon be pitted.

Opposite *The humpy nose of this 109 reveals its Spanish origin. Shipped to Spain in kit form during the war, the aircraft were assembled several years later by the Hispano company which fitted them with Merlin engines.*

Right *We eventually got them all together if only for a couple of days: all the world's flying 'Buchones' over Duxford (from top to bottom: Nick Grace in G.BOML, Walther Eichorn in D-FEHD and Reg Hallam in G-HUNN). Walther had taken ten days off for filming* Piece of Cake. *He spent seven of them fogbound in Belgium.*

This prototype first flew from the Bayerische Flugzeugwerke airfield at Augsburg-Haunstetten in May 1935, piloted by Flugkapitan 'Bubi' Knotsch. After initial factory trials it was flown to the *Erprobungsstelle* (test centre) at Rechlin, where its undercarriage collapsed on landing. It was a portent for the future, because the Me 109's narrow-track landing gear, which placed the aircraft's weight on its fuselage rather than on its lightly constructed wings, caused the 109 to wallow badly on rough surfaces and made it prone to upset if a swing developed on take-off or landing. This Achilles' Heel remained with the Messerschmitt throughout its life, perhaps

Opposite *What a* Rotte! *Reg Hallam (nearest camera) and Walther Eichorn over Cambridgeshire in Me 109s.*

Below *Kellaway (David Horovitch).*

five per cent of the 35,000-plus manufactured being destroyed in ground handling accidents.

The Me 109 and Heinkel He 112 emerged as favourites in the first rounds of a fighter selection contest held in October 1935. The following autumn the Jumo-engined second prototype Me 109V2 was flown by test pilot Hermann Wurster in the final 'play-off' against the rival Heinkel design. Wurster started a spin at 16,000 feet, making 38 turns, left, right, left, right, before recovering and climbing back to 24,000 feet for a climactic terminal velocity dive which ended near ground level. It was a compelling demonstration which may have played some small part in the Reichsluftfahrtministerium's decision to adopt Messerschmitt's design as the Luftwaffe's standard fighter aeroplane.

The first Me 109B, C and D models were blooded in combat with the Condor Legion during the Spanish Civil War, but the version against which Fighter Command fought in 1939/40 was the Me 109E 'Emil' (Willi Messerschmitt's second name) with which the Luftwaffe began a fever-pitch re-equipment programme throughout the spring and summer of 1939. The pace of Luftwaffe growth may be gauged from the knowledge that in the first nine months of the year Messerschmitt and subcontractors Erla Maschinenwerk and Fieseler Werke built 1,091 Emils, against the 450 Luftwaffe fighters delivered from *all* manufacturers in the whole of 1938.

The Me 109E differed from earlier models in having a 1,175 hp fuel-injected Daimler-Benz DB 601A engine. Small and light, it climbed at more than 3,000 feet per minute and had a maximum speed of 354 mph around 16,000 feet – slower than the

Spitfire despite having more power. But unlike the RAF's Spitfire it was available to the Luftwaffe in substantial numbers from the outset of war.

Towards the end of 1939 the definitive Me 109E-3 was in production. This most common of all Emil sub-variants was powered by an uprated DB 601A engine and was armed with five guns – two 7.9 mm Rheinmetall MG 17 machine guns mounted on top of the engine cowling, two wing-mounted 20 mm Mauser MG DD cannon, and a single cannon firing through the propeller hub, though this was rarely fitted in combat because of the severe vibration that resulted when it was fired.

The Emil drew first blood against the RAF on 4 September 1939 when an Me 109E-1 of II/JG 77 shot down a No. 9 Squadron Vickers Wellington bomber which was attempting an attack on the battleships *Scharnhorst* and *Gneisenau* at Brunsbuttel. Three months later a mixed force of Me 109Bs, Cs and Es destroyed half of a formation of 24 Wellingtons raiding the port of Wilhelmshaven on 18 December, for the loss of two Me 109s. During the Phoney War on the Western Front Emils skirmished infrequently with Allied fighters, but such encounters as there had been were sufficient to persuade Adolf Galland that 'antiquated Hurricanes ... could do little against our new Me 109E. We outstripped them in speed, rate of climb, armament and above all, in flying experience and training.'

No wonder Reichsmarschall Hermann Goering felt sure of his Luftwaffe's ability to deal summarily with the RAF when it launched the attack on Britain; indeed Me 109s accounted for most of the 1,172 British aircraft lost in the Battle of Britain, though the con-

fident plan to overwhelm Britain's defences was foiled.

Argument still rages as to which was the best of the Battle of Britain fighters. On balance the Spitfire and Me 109E were more or less evenly matched, each with its share of pluses and minuses. Among the latter the Emil had a less than ideal cockpit, small, cramped for a tall pilot, and enclosed by a fussily framed sideways-hinging canopy which restricted vision and could not be opened in flight to

improve outlook in the airfield circuit when landing. On take-off the Me 109's narrow-track landing gear demanded sensitive footwork and a gentle throttle hand to prevent a catastrophic swing developing, but the powerful lightweight fighter was quickly aloft. Climb-out and prolonged flight at high speed and power settings were leg-tiring because the Emil had no rudder trim to counteract torque – a curious omission. At high speed the Emil's aileron forces became so heavy that rolling required great strength, while pitch forces increased to the point that recovery from a high speed dive could only be made very gently, which was perhaps as well because the aircraft had a record of structural failure in the wings and tail unit, the latter featuring long obsolescent external strut bracing.

The Emil's assets? It could be racked into a tight turn at low airspeed with less fear of stalling or spinning out, thanks to its British-invented Handley Page leading edge slats, which also enabled it to climb slowly and steeply when needed, making it difficult for pursuing British pilots to keep it sighted. However, as the slats popped in and out they yawed the aircraft, and set up a weathercocking motion which was not conducive to accurate gun-aiming.

Perhaps the Me 109's greatest advantage was the Daimler-Benz engine's direct fuel injection system which enabled Luftwaffe pilots to escape a pursuer by pushing over into a steep dive – 'wide-open throttles and eyes bulging,' recalled Adolf Galland. The carburettors of Rolls-Royce Merlins would briefly starve the engine of fuel in such a manoeuvre, so Spitfire and Hurricane pilots developed the technique of half-rolling into a dive, keeping positive g forces on the fuel system, then half-rolling erect again;

Right *Anything you can do I can do lower . . .*
Spitfires beat up Charlton Park, May 1988.

Opposite *'Skull' (Richard Hope).*

Below *Ray Hanna flies his Spitfire under Winston bridge. At first we thought this scene would have to be created by deft editing or computer animation – until Ray said that, given a flyable bridge, he would do it for real. Finding a flyable bridge took months. Safety demanded that it could not be on a busy road or too close to houses and people, and it had to have a long, straight run in for the Spitfire. Winston bridge in Co. Durham is the largest single-span stone bridge in Britain – but at 200 mph the 100 ft semi-circle is a fearsomely tiny target.*

Anticlockwise from top
Nick Grace attacks the back of the Harvard trainer: the Spitfire-like tail of the Harvard made it a useful camera ship for combat shots.

Spitfires with a real combat history: ML417 and MH434 both have kills to their name.

Night shooting near Charlton Park: the wrecked Heinkel wreathed in stage mist.

Smoke is blown over Tom Burlinson in the cockpit rig at Elstree; the director monitors the shot on video.

Right *Fifty years on – 'Hoof' Proudfoot victory rolls a MkI Spitfire over the cliffs at Friston, Sussex.*

Below *Spitfire MkXI PL983 over Duxford and Hispano Messerschmitt G-BOML taxiing at Charlton.*

As Piece of Cake's *Hornet Squadron spends more than six months in France, the unit had to film at the location twice: in February to shoot the winter scenes and in May for the spring and early autumn scenes.*
Above *Golden afternoon light reflects off the house and a replica Spitfire on the first day of filming in February.*
Right *At the end of shooting in May, three Spitfires take off, leaving the replicas to be derigged and moved to the next location.*

Winter afternoon skies lent an extraordinary atmosphere to flying sequences too. In February most of the flying had to be filmed towards the end of the day when the crosswind dropped enough to make takeoff and landing possible on the small strip.

Rivalling the Spitfire in elegance, Michael Astor's de Havilland Dominie lands past the house at Charlton Park.

Spitfire over Charlton Park.

Takeoff at South Cerney.

but the time needed to complete the manoeuvre inevitably increased a Messerschmitt pilot's chance of escaping.

Despite a production run which exceeded 35,000 aircraft of all variants, only 15 genuine German-built Messerschmitt Me 109s are known still to exist, and none is currently in airworthy condition.

In 1942, however, Germany had reached agreement with Spain's Ministerio del Aire for licence manufacture of the Me 109. Delays in deliveries of jigs, tools, engines and armament prevented any Spanish aircraft being built in wartime, but post-war Hispano Aviación at Seville developed a series of Me 109-based aircraft for the Ejército del Aire using

Hispano-Suiza and – with a nice touch of irony – Rolls-Royce Merlin power plants. Known as the HA-1112-M1L Buchon (a breed of Spanish pigeon), this aircraft remained in production until 1958, by which time Hispano had built 239 Me 109s, 170 of them with Merlin engines. Buchones served with Ala 47 de Misiones Varias and Ala 36 Mixta squadrons of the Spanish Air Force until 1967, when 27 single-seat HA-1112-M1Ls and one two-seat HA-1112-M4L trainer variant were acquired for filming *The Battle of Britain*, subsequently forming the nucleus of airworthy 'Me 109s' in warbird collections in Britain and the United States.

For *Piece of Cake* three of these

Below A notoriously tricky aircraft. The Me 109 has a fearsome reputation for ground looping and landing accidents. Walther Eichorn gets airborne in D-FEHD at Duxford.

Merlin-engined Hispano HA-1112-M1L Buchons were used, suitably painted to represent early wartime Emils.

D-FEHD, based at Mannheim in Germany, is owned by Hans Dittes and flown by Walter Fritz Eichorn. Recovered from the Spanish Air Force, it was restored with the help of two former Messerschmitt engineers and first flew again in the autumn of 1986. Walter Eichorn spent an afternoon with top-scoring 352-victory Luftwaffe ace Erich Hartmann before making the first flight. D-FEHD is usually painted to represent an Me 109G Gustav of III/JG 54 Grunherz (Green Heart) squadron, Luftwaffe.

G-BOML, recently restored by Sussex-based engineer and pilot Nick Grace, was among the 28 Buchons gathered for filming *The Battle of Britain* in 1968. Subsequently sold in the United States, it was retrieved by Nick Grace, and its extensive rebuild was completed in the spring of 1988. G-BOML joins a two-seat Mk 9 Spitfire in the Grace collection.

G-HUNN is another *Battle of Britain* veteran which was also retrieved from the United States and restored in 1982 for warbirds enthusiast Robs Lamplough. It succumbed to the Messerschmitt penchant for ground-looping on landing during a display at Biggin Hill and was sold to Paul Raymond for his Theatre of War in London. After the theatre's demise, Hampshire-based collector Charles Church acquired it, and his team of engineers completed restoration in the summer of 1988, just in time for its role in *Piece of Cake*.

Heinkel He 111

Conceived to serve dual roles as a high-speed transport for the German airline Lufthansa and as a fast bomber for the clandestine Luftwaffe, the twin-engined Heinkel He 111 was the work of the twin brothers Gunter: Walter a gifted mathematician, Siegfried artistically inclined, as reflected by the streamlined cigar profile and sweeping curves of the aeroplane.

Bomber and transport prototypes flew within 16 days of each other in February and March 1934. The production He 111B bomber, powered by two supercharged 950 hp Daimler-Benz DB 600 engines, was thought by the Luftwaffe to be the best tactical bomber in the world. Capable of speeds up to 230 mph, it proved in combat with the Condor Legion in Spain quite able to evade intercepting fighters by speed alone, leading Hermann Goering and his Luftwaffe colleagues to conclude, erroneously, that large formations of fast medium bombers would be invincible.

The most prolific version of 'Die Spaten' (Spade), as the He 111 was nicknamed by its crews, was the He 111H, which first flew in 1939. It combined the preceding He 111P's characteristic multi-faceted fully glazed 'hall of mirrors' nose (a reflecting, misting nightmare for pilots), with offset ball and ventral 'bathtub' gun turrets with 1,200 hp Jumo 211 engines, whose unique throbbing, unsynchronised note was a sure herald to the

First Kill. This Spanish-built Heinkel 1-11 had lain for many years in bits in a coal yard near Cambridge before Aces High resurrected it for Piece of Cake.

British people of imminent arrival of 'Jerry bombers' as waves of Heinkel He 111s spearheaded the *blitzkrieg*.

The first major attack by Heinkels was launched on 15 August 1940 when 63 He 111s from KG 26 based at Stavanger, Norway attacked RAF Dishforth and Linton-on-Ouse in Yorkshire, losing eight aircraft to the defending Spitfires of 41, 72 and 607 squadrons. On 5 September He 111s from KG 2, KG 3, KG 26, KG 53 and KG 55 were decimated by no fewer than 14 RAF fighter squadrons scrambled to intercept their raids on London Docks and Croydon, the German crews having been led to believe that Fighter Command would offer little resistance. In truth, a competent pilot of any modern fighter of the day could effortlessly despatch the lightly armed He 111.

After the Battle of Britain the ageing Spaten was used mostly for night raids, but continued to soldier on until the end of the war, progressively gaining more defensive armament and weight, losing speed, but ably fulfilling many

operational roles for which it had not originally been intended, such as torpedo bomber, troop transport and glider tug. More than 7,000 were built, and like the Me 109, the Heinkel was manufactured in Spain after the war. Construcciones Aeronauticas S.A. (CASA) manufactured 200 He 111H-6s, known in Spain as the CASA 2111, between 1945 and 1956. Most were built or later fitted with a pair of Rolls-Royce Merlin engines. CASA 2111s were used as day bombers, reconnaissance bombers, transports and multi-engine trainers. Some remained in service until the late 1960s and, like the Spanish Air Force's Buchons, figured prominently in *The Battle of Britain*.

One such aircraft, G-AWHB, was used for static scenes in *Piece of Cake*. A former exhibit at the now defunct Historic Aircraft Museum at Southend Airport, it was auctioned in 1983 to Paul Raymond's Theatre of War, and again to the Weeks Air Museum in Florida, but was held in store at Royston, Hertfordshire from where

Aces High Limited acquired it for use in *Piece of Cake*. The CASA 2111 used for the flying sequences is owned by the Confederate Air Force in Harlingen, Texas, home of the world's largest collection of flyable wartime aircraft. Once General Franco's personal transport, it is one of the few bombers of the period equipped with a flush lavatory.

B-25 Mitchell

The camera ship used for shooting the aerial sequences in *Piece of Cake* was a North American B-25 Mitchell, owned by aviation film specialists Aces High Ltd. The twin-engined Mitchell, named after General William 'Billy' Mitchell, staunch but controversial proponent of American air power in the 1920s, served as a medium bomber with the United States Army Air Force and the Royal Air Force during World War Two. It is best remembered as the aircraft which General James Doolittle flew when he led a 16-plane surprise raid on Tokyo on 18 April 1942 after taking off from the deck of the aircraft carrier USS *Hornet*.

Opposite *Bearing the markings of a German World War Two search and rescue and casualty transport aircraft, this Spanish-built version of the Junkers Ju52 made a brief appearance in* Piece of Cake. *(Picture taken over the English Channel by aerial cameraman Simon Werry from the Castleair helicopter.)*

Below *Pilot Maker MkII – Old Flying Machine Company's Harvard trainer is still being used to train pilots to fly more powerful piston-engined fighters. The rear cockpit canopy has been removed for the camera installation.*

Aces High's B-25, which arrived at the company's base at North Weald, Essex in early April, has an interesting history. It was formerly owned by Tallmantz Aviation of Santa Ana, California, founders of the now-defunct Movieland of the Air Museum at Orange County Airport. Tallmantz Aviation was formed by the celebrated movie stunt pilots Paul Mantz, who died in an accident in 1965 while filming *The Flight of the Phoenix*, and the late Frank Tallman. Mantz was quick to see the potential of the B-25 as a camera ship. He bought his first, nicknamed 'The Smasher', in the mid-1950s and adapted it with a special optically corrected nose section for Cinerama cameras in place of the standard 'Crystal Palace' multi-pane glazed nose of the Mitchell bomber. Mantz and his close friend Darryl Zanuck took 'The Smasher' on a round-the-world flight during 1957 to shoot Lowell Thomas's *Seven Wonders of the World*. The trip included a notorious zero-feet 'beat up' of the beach at Cannes.

N1042B also has the Tallmantz optical nose section, and appeared on the other end of the camera lens – along with 17 other B-25s – in the 1970 Paramount production of Joseph Heller's novel *Catch 22*.

SETTING THE SCENE

How the aircraft and locations were found

Robert Eagle

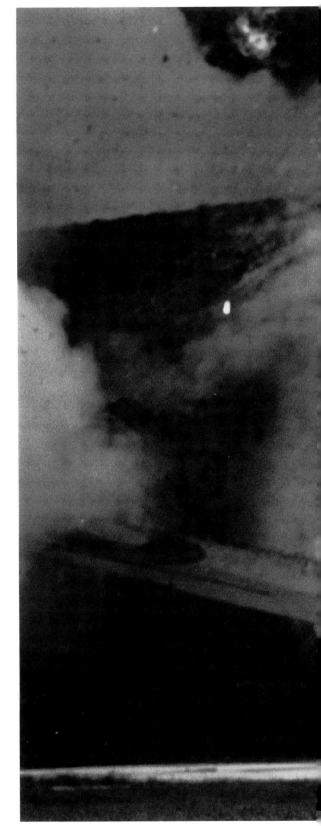

Early on, long before *Piece of Cake* was commissioned, we actually considered building our own aircraft for the production. We learned that an American was selling plans for ⅝th-scale Hurricane replicas and that a few of these replicas had actually been built. An aircraft restorer quoted us £30,000 a piece for constructing a squadron of these mini-fighters. This seemed a good idea until we saw a picture of one of the 'Hurricanes' which had been built in the USA. It was equipped with a bulbous flat four engine which ruined the sleek, narrow line of the aircraft's nose.

We also considered the idea of using Hurricanes for the episodes when the squadron is based in France, then switching to Spitfires for the latter part of the story when the squadron is based in England, but still there would have been too few to mount a credible show. Spitfires were the only option.

As Mike Jerram mentions, there are about 160 Spitfires in existence; but very few of these are airworthy and even fewer were any good for us. To retain, as far as possible, the look of the 1939–40 period, we only wanted the early 'high back' Spitfires. Later models of the Spitfire had bubble canopies and the longer Griffon engine, and though more numerous, were not right for this early period of the war.

Most of the Spitfires we eventually used were fitted with cannon on their wings. Again, this is not strictly accurate for the period, as the first Spitfires only carried machine guns which were built into the wing. Only two of the aircraft we used had the smooth un-cluttered wing of those early Spitfires. But as it would have cost about £20,000 to remove the cannon and then replace them – a job which involves taking the wings apart – we took the aircraft as they came. All our static replica Spitfires were in fact modelled on Ray Hanna's Mk IX.

Ray Hanna was the obvious choice as chief pilot for *Piece of Cake*. A former leader of the RAF Red Arrows display team, Ray has an ardent following as an airshow pilot and is renowned for his dramatic low flying which he first learnt flying Meteor jets in the 1950s. His son Mark, an RAF Phantom pilot, was deputy chief pilot.

The Hannas' Old Flying Machine Company operates a small squadron of World War Two aircraft. The Hannas and their team of pilots also flew the two Spitfires provided by collector Doug Arnold for *Piece of Cake*, and

A couple of gallons of petrol and a naphthalane burster make good work of £20,000 worth of replica Spitfire at Charlton Park.

'Moggy' Cattermole (Neil Dudgeon).

Stephen Grey flew the Mk IX Spitfire from his Fighter Collection. The fifth Spitfire was flown by 'Hoof' Proudfoot, a former RAF fighter combat instructor who–like most of the *Piece of Cake* pilots–now earns his living as an airline captain.

Painting the aircraft called for further compromises between period accuracy and budget constraints. During the first year of the war, paint schemes changed several times. Purists will protest, for instance, that we should have had simple red and blue roundels on the sides of the fuselage, and black and white undersurfaces to the wings for the French episodes. However, as our flying sequences were not filmed in the same order as they appear on the screen, it would have been extremely tiresome, time-consuming and expensive to repaint the aircraft constantly. So we opted for an early 1940 Spitfire scheme which served for the entire twelve-month period covered by *Piece of Cake*.

For the same reason we decided to drop squadron identification codes after the aircraft had departed for France in the first episode. These are the large letters on the side of the fuselage. Each code consists of three letters, a two-letter code to identify the squadron and a third letter identifying the individual aircraft. We had a large batch of letters made up in Fablon. Although they look realistic on the aeroplanes, these letters proved a nightmare for the film-maker. Not only did they have to be changed between each shot to ensure that each pilot in each scene appeared in his own aircraft, they also had the tendency to fly off in mid-air. Worse still, bits of letters would disintegrate, leaving the aircraft looking as if it was covered in Russian or Hebrew script. These problems cost us a lot of lost filming

and flying time. We were all glad to see the back of them – and to hell with the purists!

Finding Spitfires was a relatively simple task compared to getting hold of German aircraft of the period. Almost all genuine German fighters and bombers from World War Two had been destroyed during or shortly after the war. When the *The Battle of Britain* film had been made almost 20 years earlier, the producers had bought a squadron of flying Messerschmitt Me 109s and a large supply of spares from the Spanish Air Force, and had been lent a flight of Spanish built Heinkel 1-11s.

After that film had been completed, almost all the Hispano Messerschmitt aircraft had been bought by wealthy Americans and exported to the USA. A few of the CASA Heinkels had also been purchased by the Americans from the Spanish government. In the intervening years most of these aircraft had been crashed or neglected. When we began hunting for aircraft for *Piece of Cake*, there was only one flying Heinkel and one flying Messerschmitt in the world, both owned by the Confederate Air Force in Texas.

The Confederate Air Force is an extraordinary organisation. Set up by a group of Texan crop sprayers and oil men, who started their collection with a single USAAF surplus Mustang fighter, the CAF is a registered charity which now owns the largest collection of World War Two aircraft in the world. And the CAF has encouraged many private collectors to donate their own valuable aircraft, which can be set off against income tax liabilities. Many are still maintained and flown by their former owners or by volunteers, who pay an annual subscription for belonging to the organisation. In return they are given the honorary title of 'colonel'.

So as well as being the only air force in the world to be staffed entirely by upper ranks, the CAF saves itself enormous operating costs.

Thanks to these savings, the CAF was able to quote less than half the price we would have had to pay for hiring such aircraft even if they were available in Europe. Furthermore, the fact that the CAF had a second Me 109 (which it was prepared to get back into airworthy condition for us) *and* an early Spitfire made us think that much of our aerial filming could be done in Texas.

Our hopes were dashed by a terrible accident. Dick Baird, one of the few CAF pilots who could fly the airworthy Me 109, crashed in the aircraft and died a few weeks before we were going out to Texas to do our first shoot. The cause of the accident is still unclear. It seems either to have been a fuel pump problem or failure of the constant speed propeller mechanism; but it happened at low level and the pilot was unable to recover before the aircraft hit the ground after ploughing through power lines.

Later, in fact, we did use the CAF's Spanish Heinkel for filming in Texas. The problem was that Texas does not look much like southern England; so the cameraman had to be careful not to let his lens drift too low in case it picked up landscape details such as the long straight roads and modern Texan towns which would have betrayed the location. We tried hard to get the Heinkel over to England, but the CAF was understandably reluctant to risk the aircraft's age and uniqueness in a two-way trip across the North Atlantic for the sake of a few hours' filming.

'Pip' Patterson (George Anton).

There was another Spanish Heinkel, however, which might have done the trip. It was owned by David Tallichet, a millionaire restaurateur based in California, who decorates his premises to look like World War Two aerodromes. A former B25 bomber pilot himself, he has a vast collection of 'warbirds'. Tallichet offered to get his Heinkel back in airworthy condition and flown over to the UK for filming for $70,000. This was an attractive idea, but the cost was three times the amount quoted for using the CAF Heinkel in Texas. Furthermore, he valued the aircraft at $400,000 and wanted us to insure it against all risks, which would have added another $30,000 or $40,000 to our costs.

Mike Woodley, the British aviation entrepreneur who later provided our B25 camera ship, offered to acquire the Heinkel from Tallichet and supply it to us at a more affordable price. Unfortunately his deal with Tallichet fell through.

Another plan which sadly came to nought was to bring a Mk VIII Spitfire, owned by Franco Actis, over from Turin. This would have given us our sixth Spitfire which we dearly wanted in order to shoot a classic twin vic formation over the south coast. Two days before the aircraft was to be flown over from Italy, Franco's son had a bad accident in a glider and the distraught owner lost all enthusiasm for the project.

Another blow was the loss of Grawhen Hornet Squadron mistakenly Bristol Blenheim, which we had hoped to use for the scene in the first episode when Hornet squadron mistakenly shoot down a Blenheim, thinking it is a Junkers 88. In one of the most painstaking restoration projects ever undertaken, the Blenheim had been rebuilt from the derelict hulk of a Canadian Bolingbroke aircraft. But during one of its first flights at an airshow at Denham in 1987, misjudged engine handling resulted in a crash landing which totally wrote the aircraft off.

Accidents such as these highlight the problems and dangers which lie in wait for any project like *Piece of Cake* which relies on these wonderful, but fragile, antiques.

... And six replica Spitfires too

Five Spitfires hardly make a squadron. Although we reckoned we would be able to get plausible aerial scenes with the few aircraft at our disposal, we would clearly need more than five Spitfires on the ground.

Apart from standing them in long rows to give the impression that Hornet Squadron was more or less up to strength, we were also faced with the problem of blowing up several aircraft. At £300,000 a throw, real Spitfires come a bit expensive – nor would the owners be too happy about it.

So it was clear that we were going to have to build a number of replica Spitfires for *Piece of Cake*. In the event, building and maintaining these replicas proved to be far more daunting than we had originally envisaged.

A few Spitfire replicas already existed. Three of the fibreglass replicas made for *The Battle of Britain* film were still in private hands – fairly remarkable considering that they were built 20 years ago to last only a couple of months. Unfortunately, two of these had been left standing outside over the years and looked pretty decrepit. Clearly we would have to start from scratch.

Sorry Doug! Special effects despatch another replica in spectacular fashion. It was cheaper than using the real thing.

Although we had originally budgeted for three replicas, it soon became apparent that we would need six. Apart from being transportable, they would be called on to perform a variety of tasks. Some would have to be sufficiently sturdy and detailed for close-up filming, with actors in the cockpit; and they needed to be mobile (or at least pushable), and to have rotating propellers so they could look like genuine aircraft preparing for takeoff. One of them had to be self-propelled, so that it could taxi on the airfields for shots that would have been too hazardous or expensive with a real Spitfire.

The rest were required merely for background dressing. In due course these three types of replica became known respectively as 'Rollers', 'Trundler' and 'Plonkers'.

Feggans Brown, the firm contracted to build the replicas, specialised in the making of props for television and

exhibitions. At our first meeting they made an impressive presentation which combined enthusiasm with sound research. Mainstays of the Feggans Brown team were Alan Brown, Brent Johnson, Richard Brown and David Brighton, who deserve enormous credit for producing replicas which – on the screen and on the ground – were virtually indistinguishable from the real thing, and were turned out in less than two months.

The replicas were built in one of the hangar-sized studios at Elstree studios. The Rollers were to be constructed of aluminium and the Trundler and

Plonkers of fibreglass. The fuselage of a Spitfire was borrowed from Nick Grace and three weeks were spent making an exact copy of it in aluminium; moulds were taken from this metal replica for casting the fibreglass versions. Feggans were only able to borrow a single port side wing, but a mirror image copy was built for the starboard wing.

Although the Rollers were of better quality, the Trundler was the most ingenious of the replicas. Constructed of fibreglass around a metal frame, it was equipped with two engines. A Honda 125cc motorcycle engine drove

the propeller, while the wheels were turned by hydraulic motors. In the nose of the aircraft was a tank containing 24 gallons of oil. Forward of the cockpit was a Yamaha 250cc engine which drove a pump that pushed the oil down the undercarriage legs towards the wheels. Each wheel had its own hydraulic motor – rather like a small, enclosed waterwheel – which was turned by the circulating oil. The aircraft could do nearly 30 mph on hard ground, but was rather slower on grass.

Ingenious though it was, the Trundler proved to be the most problematic

Above *The Spitfire replica construction crew had to work so late – often till 3 a.m. – patching up their handiwork for the next day's shoot – that they opted for living on site in an old bus. The dogs didn't seem to mind the cramped quarters.*

Opposite *Replica Spitfire and genuine soldiers from South Cerney stood in as ground crew and played the part like naturals.*

of the bunch. It was originally intended for a shot in which Pip Patterson's Spitfire came off the runway and ploughed into a field. All seemed to be in working order but when the time came for the shot, it suddenly packed up. The main problem was that it rapidly overheated. The aircooled engine was enclosed in the nose and got little air to cool it. Indeed, on one occasion the engine driving the propeller, after it had been turning for ten minutes or so, burst into flames which had to be put out by the halon extinguishers mounted in the nose.

The first replica to be blown up was a Roller. It would have been more economical to use a Plonker, but as the scene called for a Spitfire to taxi into the side of a wooden dispersal hut at the Charlton Park location, it had to have a rotating propeller. To get the shot, the Roller was hitched up to a towing wire which was passed under the hut and attached to the back of the special effect team's four-wheel drive truck. Oil had been poured over the grass alongside the hut to make the Spitfire slip and slide. On cue the propeller was started, the driver leapt out, and the truck pulled the replica into the side of the hut.

So far so good; but the aircraft had to explode as well. The special effects department had fitted a plastic tank with two gallons of petrol in the nose. A cortex fuse was wrapped around the tank, which was also rigged with a 'burster' containing naphthalene. As the replica hit the side of the hut, the cortex was set off by radio control, exploding the burster which vapourised and ignited the petrol. The flames leapt 40 feet.

It says something for the sturdy quality of the replicas that this Roller was refurbished within a few days and hauled down to the next location at Friston. In all, the replicas were assembled, taken apart and reassembled six times, moving from Elstree to Charlton Park, next to Cambridge, then to South Cerney, back to Charlton Park and finally to Friston. Apart from the wear and tear they inevitably suffered from being built and rebuilt, shoved around muddy fields and stood on by actors

and extras, they were a magnet for souvenir hunters, who pinched at least a dozen of the cockpit gunsights. If you are ever offered a fibreglass Spitfire gunsight, there's a fair chance it came from *Piece of Cake*.

The locations – echoes from the past

Location hunting for the series presented similar problems of authenticity and others, less predictable, into the bargain.

One evening in May 1988, after the unit had been wrapped for the day, associate producer Adrian Bate and director Ian Toynton visited a church-yard in Gloucestershire in search of a location for the funeral scene when Dicky Starr is buried after crashing his Spitfire into the bridge at Thionville. It was one of a number of sites shortlisted by location manager Mike Hook. As the scene was set in France, the church

Above *The smoke of a hundred rubber tyres wafts over Charlton Park. The wind shifted several times that day, leaving the residents wondering if they were watching a bombing raid or being the victims of one.*

Left *The replica Spitfires were modelled from Ray Hanna's MkIX. The rear view mirrors became a favourite target of thieving souvenir hunters.*

could not look typically English; and of course there had to be a suitably positioned plot where we might be allowed to dig our grave and shoot the scene.

Apart from the difficulty of finding a French-style church in England's West Country, there was the question of local sensibilities. A graveside scene can easily cause offence, and any rector is likely to be wary of a film company which asks if it can borrow his churchyard.

'The location was perfect,' Adrian recalls. 'It was a lovely little Norman church. They walked round the churchyard to find the best place where they could dig the grave and which would also give a good angle on the church.

'We found the ideal spot – but then we noticed something which made us shiver. The tombstone on the nearest grave carried the insignia and motto of the RAF. It was the grave of an RAF fighter pilot who had died in a flying accident two years earlier. It was a chilling coincidence, and we walked from the churchyard feeling very uneasy.' A different location was found for the scene.

Location hunting does not always stir such unsettling vibrations, although in many of the places where we filmed *Piece of Cake* we were deliberately seeking echoes of the past.

The location which everyone thought would be the most difficult to find – the French château at 'St Pierre' – turned out to be one of the easiest. No one had seriously entertained the hope of discovering a period country house which would pass for French and happen to have an airfield close by. It was assumed that we would have to shoot the château and airfield scenes quite separately.

Mike had been taken to tea at Charlton Park by his father a couple of years earlier. It could hardly have been better. The mansion, near Malmesbury in Wiltshire, is Jacobean, built of yellow Cotswold stone; and if it does not look typically French, it certainly doesn't look typically English either. As Stephen Grey commented: 'A bit over-egged to be really English.'

What made Charlton Park an ideal St Pierre, however, was that it had a runway leading almost all the way up to its front door. Its owner, the Earl of Suffolk, was mad keen on aeroplanes.

Some years previously Lord Suffolk had moved his family from the big house into less imposing but more amenable and comfortable quarters in the former stud farm. The mansion had been converted into apartments. Thanks to the owner's persuasive skills, the residents of the apartments

Charlton Park after the raid. The exploded 'roller' is lodged in the side of the dispersal hut. The duckboards were a hangover from the February shoot when the ground had been a quagmire.

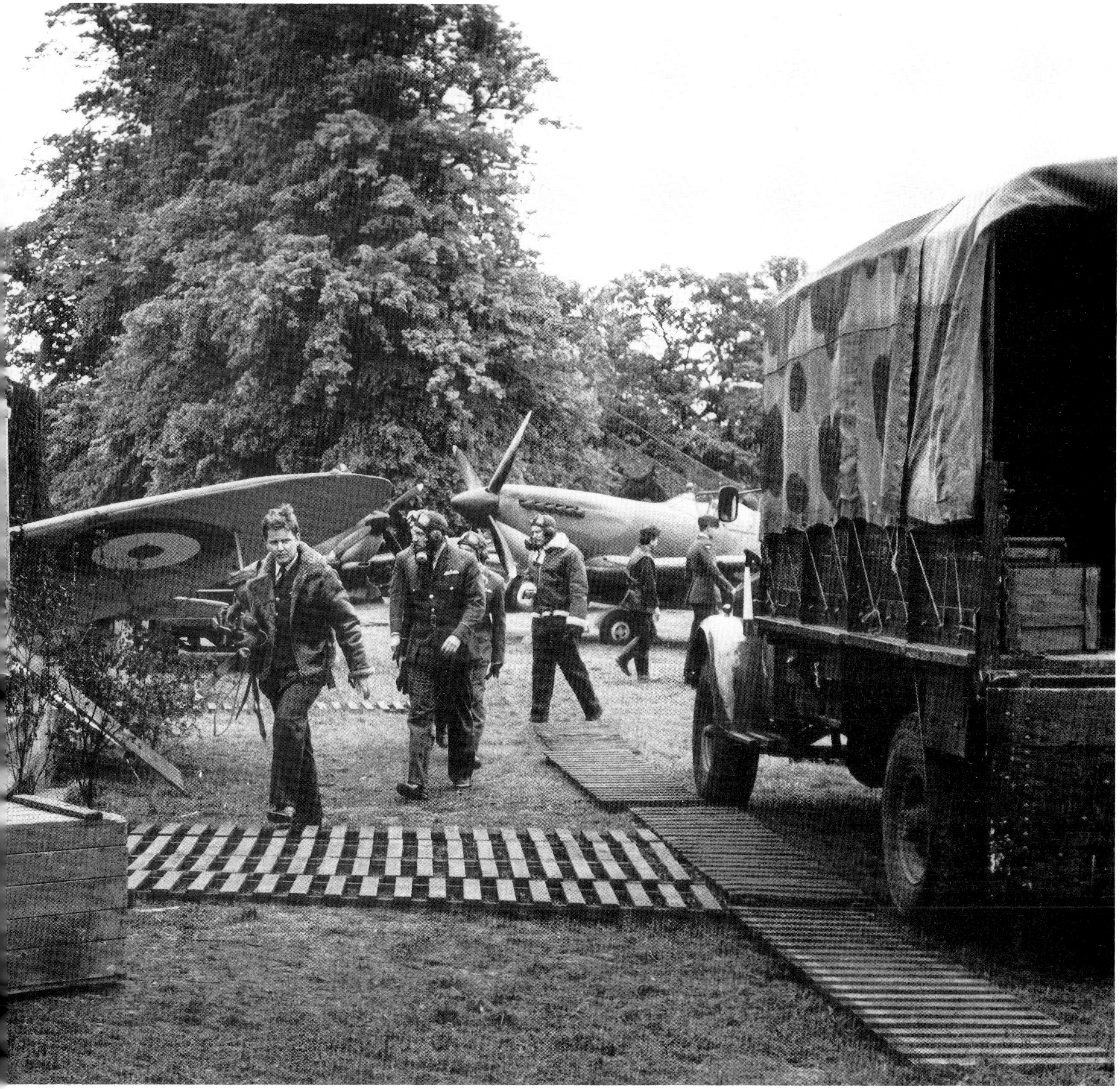

were won over to the idea of having a film crew camping in front of their home for several weeks. Although a few were somewhat disgruntled by the disruptions caused by the filming (perhaps understandably so when the special effects team got to work blowing up the set and sent clouds of black smoke billowing across the house),

most were excited at the prospect of Spitfires landing in front of the drawing room windows.

Although it was 600 yards long and 25 yards wide, the runway had to be extended for our aircraft. Ideally, Spitfire pilots like to have a 1,000-yard run; and as we aimed to have up to three Spitfires taking off at the same

Opposite *Friston: art director Jane Coleman re-created the airfield to what it must have looked like in 1942 when hundreds of airmen lived there under canvas.*

Below *Friston – 360° of nothing but rolling downs and sky.*

time, we had to double the runway's width as well. A figure was agreed to compensate Lord Suffolk for loss of crops which would otherwise have grown there, and seed for the new runway was sown in late September in the hope that we would be able to use it in the spring.

In November Ray Hanna flew his Spitfire into Charlton Park for a press day. It had been raining solidly for days and Ray, with typical understatement, muttered that the ground was 'pretty marginal'. In fact his Spitfire had bogged down while parking and it took eight men to shift it from its rut. By February, when our first filming began, it was still pretty marginal. The new part of the runway was still soft and

unusable; in fact, any aircraft trying to land on it would have nosed over. The old runway was firmer but still quite soggy and slippery. To make matters worse, for the first three days of that week a northerly wind blew at 20 knots straight across the runway, making any attempt to land even more hazardous. Several times the pilots approached the field, even managing to touch their wheels on the grass, but decided it was too risky and put down at RAF Lyneham. Finally, on the evening of 24 February, when the wind had dropped just before sunset, Mark Hanna successfully landed the first Spitfire.

By May, when we returned for filming at Charlton, the transformation was astonishing. The ground had dried

out, the grass had grown and the new runway was firm.

Using Charlton Park to represent a French château called for a little artistic licence. By contrast, the airfield we created at Friston on the Sussex coast was an authentic historical reconstruction. Gayle's Farm at Friston was the site of an actual wartime airfield which had first been used by the military in 1936. Later in the war it was an emergency landing field for aircraft limping back home across the English Channel, and occasionally served as a base for Hurricane and Spitfire squadrons. At one time more than 1,500 RAF and WAAF personnel had been stationed at Friston, most of them living in tents, perched 300 feet above the Channel and a few hundred yards from the Seven Sisters cliffs.

After the war Friston was briefly used as a glider site, but the field reverted to agriculture and eventually lost all traces of its RAF past. When our production manager, Jack Wright, came across it again in 1988, it was sporting a crop of peas.

Considering how many airfields there had been on the south coast during the war, it proved surprisingly difficult to find one which suited our purposes. We needed a grass airfield close to the sea. The majority of old airfields, in fact, lay a few miles inland and many of them, like Friston, had disappeared. Active airfields were no good to us as we had to have complete control of the location; the last thing we wanted was a Cessna taxiing into shot or into the back of our catering truck.

Although we had map references for the site of the old airfield, farming activity had all but eradicated any sign of the former runway. Ben Gunn, manager of Shoreham airport, gave us a lead; he had flown Spitfires out of Friston and remembered that the runway ran north-east/south-west. Old aerial reconnaissance pictures showed that there was a filled-in chalkpit at the southern end of the field where the runway ran towards the cliffs. Surveyors confirmed, too, that the piece of field we thought to be the old runway was indeed the flattest stretch.

Anthony Olliphant, the farmer, was somewhat amused by the notion of a

Bodkin Hazel dispersal area in the long hot summer of 1940 – shot at Friston during the not-so-flaming June of 1988.

film company flying Spitfires off his field, but was quite happy to grow grass instead of peas.

The clifftop location was ideal, but to become an airfield again the site needed a great deal of work. The ground was a mass of clods and sharp flints, any one of which could have punctured an aircraft tyre. A contractor had to be hired to remove the stones before the grass could be sown.

Fortunately, another potential hazard had already been dealt with by the Army. Like many military locations, Friston had been mined by our side and bombed by the other side during the war, and there was still plenty of high explosive underfoot, awaiting its moment of glory. Just before we began our work on the field, the Army had completed its long overdue bomb disposal task. When the field was ploughed, Jake found an old Spitfire cannon shell case in the rubble.

Seed was sown in early October, but by April, only six weeks before filming was due to start at Friston, the field still looked terrible. The grass was patchy and the contractor's machine had failed to get rid of thousands of small flints. One shuddered to think what might happen if one of these objects, sharp as a Stone Age knife, were flicked up by a propeller and projected towards the skulls of the camera crew. So the farmer was asked to seed and roll the field again, and 30 stone-pickers were recruited from the Eastbourne job centre to scour the terrain by hand. With a little help from nature, the work paid off; a month later the runway was as good as it had been 50 years earlier.

For *Piece of Cake*'s art director, Jane Coleman, Friston was a challenging location. It was an absolutely bare site.

Above *L/AC Todd (Neil Clark).*

Opposite *Spot the replica: three real Spitfires on parade at South Cerney with four replicas. South Cerney is a classic early World War Two airfield: 300 acres of grass with a perimeter track.*

Unlike Charlton Park, dominated by its big house and elegant avenue of trees, Friston offered 360° of nothing but rolling downs and sky. To create an authentic temporary RAF camp, she had three 'spider huts' (the kind of wooden shed still to be seen in old hospitals and schools in less prosperous corners of the country) and a Nissen hut built on the field. The only other dressing for the set was scores of tents, which would have been home, year in, year out, for the other ranks and a dozen splendid old RAF vehicles, including a bowser, ambulance,

fire truck and little 'Tilly' runabout vans.

By coincidence, the arrival of our replica Spitfires at Friston at the end of May 1988 echoed events at the airfield exactly 46 years earlier. On 31 May 1942 a squadron of dummy Spitfires had arrived at Friston on trucks and had been assembled on the site as a decoy for the Luftwaffe. (The Luftwaffe was not deceived. It ignored the field completely until a couple of months later when it bombed a Nissen hut and strafed a damaged Hurricane – a real one this time – on the ground.)

Hornet Squadron had of course enjoyed rather more luxurious accommodation during their posting in France. The indoor scenes at Château St Pierre were not, in fact, shot at Charlton Park but at another stately home much closer to our production base at Elstree.

Wrotham Park, near Potters Bar, is a vast mansion in the classical style which was built by the wealthy but unfortunate Admiral John Byng, who after a defeat at the hands of the French was ordered to be shot by firing squad on his own quarterdeck.

The rooms at Wrotham Park are full of 18th-century furniture and its walls are hung with extremely valuable paintings. Its owners help to keep the place going by hiring it out to conference organisers and film companies. Considering the worth of the antiques on display, they were remarkably relaxed about what we planned to do. In one of the most visually dramatic scenes, for example, the château and airfield are bombed during the wedding reception given for two of the young pilots and their brides. To create the effect of a bomb going off outside the room where the reception is being held, two large windows were removed and replaced with sugar glass. A pair of blast machines were erected outside the windows and, on the cue, a mass of cork and fuller's earth debris was flung through the windows into the room and over the assembled cast. A silent witness to this mayhem was a painting by Titian, estimated value £1 million, which was allowed to remain in place on the wall, protected by a thin cotton sheet.

Our fourth major location was another airfield which had to represent 'Kingsmere', an RAF station in Essex, from which Hornet Squadron departs for France. Jake Wright found the ideal location just 12 miles from Charlton Park. South Cerney is an aviator's dream; a classic early World War Two aerodrome, it is a 300-acre grass field encircled by an oval perimeter track, with four large hangars and a white, flat-roofed 1930s' control tower. Used as a training school, it had never been provided with hard runways, and was therefore ideal for the Spitfires which could simply line themselves up into the wind and take off in the most favourable direction.

The RAF gave up using South Cerney in 1969. It is now base for a Royal Corps of Transport regiment, and the field itself serves only for gliders at weekends and for the occasional military parachute-dropping exercise – a sad waste. But the Army could hardly have been more helpful; filming would provide an interesting diversion. The second-in-command, Major Peter Everingham, suggested that we might like to use some of his men as extras. The soldiers were perfect for the job. They looked right, they marched right and we didn't have to shell out a fortune getting their hair cut. They were always ready to help with the chore of pushing Spitfires, and they were sadly missed later.

ACTION!

How *Piece of Cake* was filmed

ROBERT EAGLE

'What are we doing in all this shit?' These are the words that will remind me most about filming *Piece of Cake*.

I am not sure which pilot said them. I was on the ground listening to the radio transmitter as five Spitfires whirled above, in and out of the clouds, pretending they were shooting the tail off a B25 bomber.

It was a typical English day in May, a brisk north-westerly wind dumping frequent showers over the airfield at Little Rissington. (The aerial unit had had to move away from the main location at South Cerney because the aircraft had been causing too much distraction for the main unit.) We had been taking advantage of a gap in the weather, but the sky was far from clear and the Spitfires, after pulling up to attack the camera ship, kept finding themselves upside down in the ragged cloud. Hence the expletive.

It is hard to say who was having the best time and the best view. The Spitfire pilots were doing what they only too rarely got the chance to do: exercise their skills at shooting hell out of a lumbering bomber. In the back of that bomber, aerial cameraman Simon Werry was enjoying his position in a way that a rear gunner never could have done; while in the midships position, second cameraman Jeff Mul-

ligan picked the Spitfires off as they overshot. Andrew Holmes, directing the aerial unit, peered out of the perspex bubble on top of the B25, and swivelled his head like an owl, shouting directions through the intercom at pilots and cameras alike. Not that they needed much encouragement; they knew what they were doing and were having a hell of a time doing it. The view from the ground was one that few in England had seen since 1940.

The next sortie was less successful, however. After attacking the B25, *Piece of Cake*'s aerial flotilla had departed for base at Duxford, with the Spitfires formating on the bomber so that the cameras could pick up some of the many formations shots we needed. Unfortunately communications between the Spitfires and the equally vintage B25 were at best never brilliant. When the B25's co-pilot decided to navigate to the north of Luton airport, the Spitfires, unable to hear her conversation with the Luton air traffic controller, who was vectoring her through the control zone, assumed she had got lost and that she was

Midships in the B25 bomber, 5,000 feet above Gloucestershire. Aerial cameraman Jeff Mulligan searches mid-sky for Spitfires.

unwittingly straying too close to the airport. The Spitfires tried to persuade the B25 to turn left by passing ahead of it a few times, then gave up and made off on their own track, leaving the cameras with nothing to shoot. As the Spitfires departed, the B25 co-pilot had to tell the Luton controller that no, the aircraft could not do a fly past down the airport runway because we were trying to get some work done up here ... and by the way could he see where all her Spitfires had gone?

Filming with aeroplanes brings excitement and frustration in equal mea-sure. Communication difficulties were a relatively minor problem. Consider-ing that the noise inside a Spitfire cockpit is like a pneumatic drill in an empty oil tank, it was a miracle that the pilots could hear themselves think, let alone communicate with formating air-craft and the camera team. The prob-lems of handling the aircraft at the filming locations were far greater.

For the director, working to a very demanding schedule, the disruption caused by landings and takeoffs was considerable. All other work would come to a halt until the Spitfires were

Above Jeff's point of view: a major problem was trying to keep yellow rape fields out of shot.

Opposite First aerial briefing: Andrew Holmes runs through the schedule with pilots Mark and Ray Hanna (standing left), the B25 team and Pete Jarvis (standing behind Holmes). Robert Eagle and Simon Werry seated foreground, left and right.

clear of the field, only to be disrupted again when they returned half an hour later. It soon became clear that the needs of the main unit and the aerial unit were incompatible. So Duxford, Little Rissington and Headcorn were used as bases for the aircraft; the planes would only be called in to the main location when we needed shots which involved actors and real aircraft.

Even when they *were* needed by the main unit, the aircraft posed major problems. It could take 40 minutes for a dozen men to push four Spitfires into the right position for a shot. If they taxied under their own power, they would overheat in ten minutes and would then have to fly or shut down for half an hour. Scenes which called for prolonged taxiing had to be shot with more than one aircraft: the first takes would be shot with one Spitfire, which would then be shut down and replaced with another to complete the scene.

Tricky winds caused further problems. While the pilots were prepared at a pinch to take off with the wind behind them, landing downwind was much more hazardous. As it was not usually feasible to suspend the action for a few days until the wind chose to blow from another quarter, some scenes had to be shot with the aircraft landing in the opposite direction to what the director wanted.

Although Leon Griffiths had taken pains not to write in too many ambitious flying sequences involving large numbers of aircraft, the potentially runaway cost of aerial shooting was always a worry.

To keep within budget Ian Toynton had storyboarded each of the flying sequences, reducing them to the bare essentials required for telling the story.

Above *Tim Woodward (Rex).*

Opposite *Elstree Studios, April 1988. Actor Tom Burlinson gets a funfair ride in the cockpit rig, while the director watches on his video monitor. The rig moved through 360° and was vibrated to ensure realism. 'It gave me a numb bum,' Tom commented.*

To ensure that the audience never lost touch with the characters who were supposed to be flying the aircraft, every second or third shot would return to the actor pilot in his cockpit.

The cockpit scenes were shot in the studio at Elstree. Two special rigs were constructed: one was the rear section of a cockpit for shots where you saw the pilot's face; the other was a forward section for shots where you were looking out of the cockpit to get the pilot's point of view. Each rig was suspended on ropes and pulleys, so that it could be swung round almost 360° to simulate banking and turning. The actor would be strapped into the rig and hoisted to the left or right, or completely inverted. These cockpit scenes were shot against a blue screen. In post-production, when the film had been transferred on to tape, the blue background was separated electronically in the video editing suite and replaced with moving shots of sky, sea or landscape.

Even with a moving background, there is always a risk that a scene shot on a studio rig will look static. In old flying films, the pilots sit stolid and motionless, as if they were set in aspic. To make our pilots look as if they were in a real aircraft, the rig and the camera platform were mechanically vibrated to give the picture – and the pilot – a realistic tremor.

For the actors these cockpit scenes were exhausting. 'Blue screen work is always a pain, physically and mentally,' Boyd Gaines commented. To hear the director above the noise of the machinery, we had to wear an earpiece under our flying helmets. At the end of the day your ears were sore.' 'And the constant vibration gave you a numb bum,' Tom Burlinson recalled.

The only effect which was too difficult to duplicate was the positive gravitational force which keeps a pilot pushed back into his seat as he loops and rolls. Upside down in the studio rig, our actor pilots were hanging in their straps. 'Trying to brace yourself back and pretend you are doing 300 mph while hanging in space is quite an effort,' Tim Woodward commented.

Whether upside down or the right way up, the actors had to keep their eyeline on the relative position of the

aircraft they were supposed to be pursuing. Boyd Gaines found this one of the most demanding tasks he had to perform on *Piece of Cake*. 'I only spent a day in the studio cockpit but I can still clearly recall where I was supposed to look for the ground, the enemy and the rest of the squadron. It was all completely imaginary, of course, but it was such hard work that every detail sticks in my mind.'

Numb bums were only one of the many privations suffered by the camera crew who did the air to air shooting. Aerial cameramen are used to hanging out of helicopters, subjected to chilly winds and heavy g forces. But in the filming of *Piece of Cake* helicopters were the cushy option.

Though *Piece of Cake*'s aerial cameramen Simon Werry and Jeff Mulli-

Above Corinne Dacla (Nicole) and Helena Michell (Mary) wait their call on location in Epping.

Opposite Friston, June 1988.

gan are two of the most cheerful people you could meet, their profession is a hazardous one and they take the risks seriously. Both have lost more friends in flying accidents than they care to count and have had bad moments of their own. Jeff fell through a hatch in a helicopter at 6,000 feet and was only saved from falling by his long 'monkey harness'. Some years earlier, during the shooting of *Catch 22*, a very experienced cameraman had been lost from the back of the B25 we were using.

The Spitfires and Messerschmitts had to be shot at different speeds, in different formations and from different angles and there was no single aircraft which could serve as a camera ship for all these tasks. The Bell Jetranger helicopter, for instance, which is one of the most popular ships for aerial filming, was simply not fast enough to keep up with a Spitfire, which at 200 knots (230 mph) is just cruising gently. We did use a Jetranger on *Piece of Cake* but only for background shots of cloud and landscape, and pilots' point-of-view shots of passing scenery. For most of the time, however, we made extensive use of the much more powerful Augusta 109 helicopter operated by Castleair. It is a twin-engined machine, and therefore inherently safer for this kind of work, especially when filming over water. Its top speed of 150 knots (a little less with the door open and a camera mount in place) – is just enough to be able to track a throttled-back Spitfire.

The great advantage of the Augusta 109 helicopter was that it could be fitted with a forward-pointing camera, so that we could get the much-needed tail-chasing shots. To achieve these, the film camera is mounted on the right-hand side of the nose of the helicopter and is operated by remote control. The cameraman is fed a video picture of what the camera is seeing and can tilt the lens as necessary from his position in the back of the helicopter. The pilot also has a video monitor to help him line up on the subject. The camera was operated at normal speed, but to make the Spitfire or Messerschmitt appear to be moving at its combat velocity of well over 300 knots, the film was played back at higher speed in post-production.

While you can shoot from the side of

Above *No detail too small: David Horovitch (Kellaway) has his artificial moustache trimmed.*

Opposite *Wardrobe mistress Lynette Cummin daubs a little artificial mud on the pilots' legs for the first scene of the series (South Cerney).*

the helicopter, or from the front with the special camera mount, you cannot point your camera directly backwards. This is where the B25 bomber and the Harvard came into their own.

The Harvard is a World War Two dual seat aircraft which was designed for training fighter pilots. As big as a Spitfire, but less streamlined and less powerful, it was the aircraft many RAF pilots moved on to after learning the basics in the Tiger Moth. It still serves a similar purpose today: because it was made to handle like a fighter of the time, it is one of the very few types on which pilots can gain useful experience before attempting to fly single seat aircraft like the Spitfire.

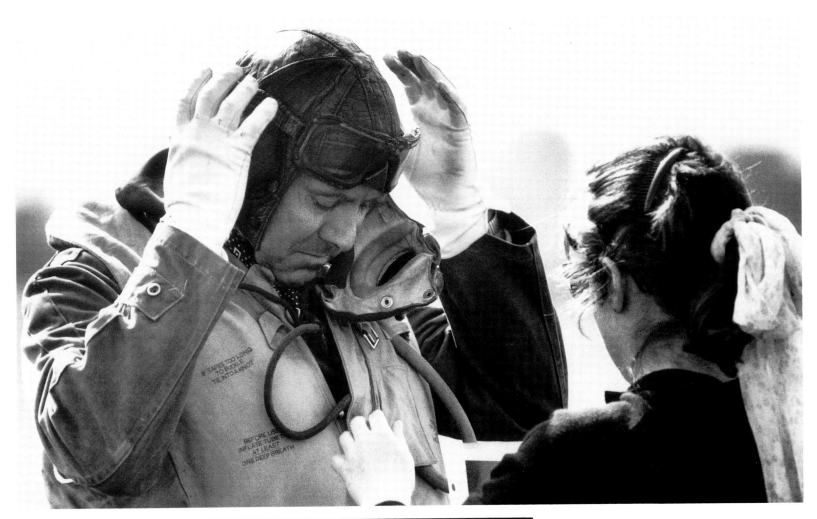

Above *Spitfire pilot Pete Jarvis being kitted out as squadron leader Ramsey for close shots. Wardrobe mistress Lynette Cummin spent weeks finding period clothing, but in the air the pilots preferred to wear more comfortable clothing.*

Left *The heat is on – Tim Woodward (Rex) is sprayed with artificial sweat at Charlton Park.*

Opposite *Ramsay (Jack McKenzie) in the cockpit.*

The pilot and instructor in a Harvard sit one behind the other under a long 'greenhouse' canopy. For our purposes the Harvard was interesting because the aft section of the canopy could be removed to allow a camera to be mounted behind the rear cockpit. Pointing backwards, a camera in this position was ideal for the other end of those tail-chasing shots: the view back to the attacking aircraft. The fact that you also got the tail of the Harvard in shot was a positive advantage, because from this angle it closely resembled the tail of a Spitfire. Using the Harvard in this way helped us to make up for the fact that we had only five Spitfires, instead of the six we would have liked to make a full flight. The tail or wingtip of the Harvard in shot gave us the sixth Spit.

For cameraman Simon Werry, who designed the special rig for the Harvard, however, this position was less than comfortable. Facing backwards on a seat which was designed for someone sitting the other way round, puts a great strain on the thighs. Frequent little shifts of position were required to prevent damage to more tender parts. Simon had never felt more in need of his monkey harness and more grateful to pilots for their ability to fly smoothly. Despite these drawbacks, he managed to get some unique shots from the Harvard; perhaps the most remarkable shot was achieved with the Harvard performing a barrel roll in formation with the pursuing aircraft.

The history of the B25 we used has already been outlined by Mike Jerram in Chapter 4. To fly the beast, its new owner, Mike Woodley, had persuaded the veteran Confederate Air Force pilot, Vernon Thorp, to come over from Florida to join us for a month. At 70 years old, Vernon is still very active

professionally as a ferry pilot and instructor. His 28-year-old co-pilot, Anita Mays, was one of the youngest professional pilots qualified to fly the B25.

Compared with a helicopter, the B25 is as spacious as a bus. This specially-adapted aircraft has six camera positions: one in the tail, one in the nose, one on the port side, two on the starboard, and one by the bomb doors in the belly. The director has his own vantage point behind the cockpit from where he can see in most directions except straight down.

Unfamiliarity with the radio and intercom system of the B25 gave us all kinds of problems at first. Sometimes the director could speak to the pilots and/or the Spitfires but not to the cameramen; at other times the cameraman in the tail could talk to the Spitfires but could hear no one else. As it was costing over £250 a minute to keep all this hardware – one bomber, five Spits and cameras, not to mention the pilots and camera crew – in the air, these problems caused a certain amount of friction until the causes of electrical problems and 'finger trouble' were identified.

Despite such hassles, filming with the B25 was a high point in the making of *Piece of Cake*. As Andrew Holmes said wistfully: 'Seeing all those Spitfires flying for us in the same colours as they would have carried in their finest hour made me think that this was perhaps our finest hour too!'

Filming aircraft is technically demanding and very expensive. It also has some quite severe limitations. The

Shooting from the ground often produced more spectacular footage than aerial filming. (Carl Schofield beating up Charlton Park in MH434.)

Below *Beyond the call of duty: one of the South Cerney soldiers gives the director a lift.*

Right *The Zero CV – the idea was that the car would track the path of an approaching Messerschmitt. The aircraft arrived on cue; the car broke down; the director bit his lip (Charlton Park).*

main problem was that, when it came to editing the material, few shots were really worth holding for more than about three seconds. If the aircraft were moving at high speed relative to the camera, three seconds was about all the time you had before they had filled the frame and passed. If they were moving slowly in relation to the camera – as, for instance, in the case of the formation shots taken from the B25 – the lack of relative speed slowed down the pace of the action. Held for too long, the aircraft had all the dramatic impact of fish in an aquarium. While the aviation buff would doubtless be happy to spend hours watching aerial shots of formating Spitfires and Messerschmitts the demands of drama were otherwise.

Indeed some of the most exciting shots of flying aircraft were taken from the ground. At Charlton Park the Spitfires passing low – very, very low – above the ground before pulling up over the house; at Friston, Spitfire and Messerschmitt jinking past the white cliffs: these were shots which will probably be best remembered from *Piece of Cake*. One of the best dogfight sequences was shot from the runway at Friston. Close proximity to the ground emphasises the speed of the aircraft and adds an immediacy, a hint of danger which is missing when the aircraft are higher in the sky. Takeoffs and landings also often make better viewing than many more ambitious aerial shots; because the aircraft are in a state of transition from one element to another, they hold your attention for longer.

Perhaps the greatest problem for the director Ian Toynton was creative rather than purely practical. Even parked on the grass, a Spitfire has considerable power and presence. 'They are so charismatic, they dominate any scene they are in. I did not want the Spitfires to upset the balance of the drama. So when we came to editing *Piece of Cake*, I tried to ensure that the audience would be left feeling they wanted to see more of the aircraft.'

The muted, romantic quality of the pictures in *Piece of Cake* must be credited to the skills of lighting cameraman Peter Jessop. The quality was enhanced by using 35 mm film in the new 'three perf' format. Most of the drama made for British television is shot on 16 mm film or videotape, both of which are considerably less expensive than 35 mm, though inferior in most other respects. 'Three perf' is a more economical 35 mm format. The frame size is slightly smaller than the conventional format; each frame is bordered by three sprocket holes or perforations instead of the conventional four. The viewer does not notice any difference in the shape of the image as about ten per cent around the border of any image is lost anyway on a domestic television set, but the picture quality is of cinematic standard.

We cannot leave the subject of filming aircraft without mentioning *Piece of Cake*'s most unexpected success in this area. At the end of the second episode a Messerschmitt flies past the French airfield and drops a chamber-pot in front of the astonished British pilots. Initially we had little hope that

Celebrating the successful potty mission. First assistant director, Jake Wright, was a Seafire pilot in WW2.

this scene could be shot as a single take. The practical problems seemed insuperable. Unlike the Spitfire with its sliding canopy, the Messerschmitt only has a small window which is difficult for the pilot to open in flight. We also doubted that the pilot would be happy to throw a solid object out of the aircraft in case it damaged the tailplane. And even if the pilot could be persuaded, the Civil Aviation Authority would have to grant a special exemption to the Air Navigation Order, which expressly forbids the dropping of objects from aircraft in flight.

However, the art department came up with a novel solution – chamberpots cast in the kind of thin plastic used in the manufacture of ping-pong balls. These were rather smaller than your average potty, but not too big to pass through the little window of the Messerschmitt. After some misgivings, the pilot, Reg Hallam, was persuaded that a 2-oz plastic potty could not do too much damage to his aeroplane, even if it did hit something on the way out. The Civil Aviation Authority seemed to agree, and granted the necessary exemption. But the question remained: would a 2-oz plastic potty sink to the ground or blow away in the slipstream? Frankly, we all thought it would blow away.

There is precious little room inside a Messerschmitt cockpit for the pilot's map, let alone a pair of potties. The only way we could get them in was to tape them on to the pilot's shoulders. This restricted Reg's ability to move his head, but as you can't see much out of a Messerschmitt cockpit anyway (however much you move your head) this was not going to cramp his style unduly. So off he went. He did one pass over the field to judge his spot. Unfortunately when he tried to open

the little window, the handle came off in his hand and he had to claw it open with his fingernails. On the next pass, as the cameras rolled, he ripped a potty off his shoulder and pushed it through the window. Instead of blowing away, it dropped in a gentle arc, hit the ground, bounced once and came to rest on the grass within ten feet of the chosen spot. *Piece of Cake.*

The sad thing is I bet half the audience thought we cheated it.

Above *Taking it philosophically: screenwriter Leon Griffiths watches the action at South Cerney.*

Opposite *More attention to detail: replica Spitfires were used for shots showing the actor pilots taxiing their aircraft. A wind machine blew air and smoke and handfuls of grass cuttings over the cockpit to simulate the prop blast and exhaust fumes. As the replica was pushed forward, the camera tracked back on its dolly.*

Fx: the special effects

It is common sense in the film business that you never get on the wrong side of a special effects man. Blood, smoke and explosions are his stock in trade, and he has many ways of exacting revenge in gory fashion. So when *Piece of Cake*'s special effects expert, Graham Longhurst, was found trussed up and yelling in the bottom of a ditch one day at Charlton Park, it seemed that someone was playing a dangerous game.

In fact someone had been taking revenge on Graham! Early that morning the Feggans Brown crew, asleep in their bus, had been woken by thick smoke wafting over their bunks. They rushed coughing and spluttering out into the fresh air, where Graham, fire hose in hand, gave them all a brisk dousing.

Practical jokes aside, Graham points out that most of the materials he uses are very safe. He needed to make a great deal of smoke for *Piece of Cake*. For white smoke his team used refined cooking oil, for black smoke they burnt old rubber tyres. 'Tyres are horrible and smelly, but they are safe and economical. The best black smoke can be toxic because it is sulphur based, and it is also very expensive. So as there were usually lots of people around, we used tyres.' And they used a great deal of them – up to 5,000 for a single day's shooting.

Right *Finger on the button: Graham Longhurst prepares for countdown for the big raid on Friston.*

Below *The Harvard acquires a rear gunner. Aerial cameraman Simon Werry designed this special rig for filming tail-chasing Messerschmitts.*

Wind can play havoc with smoke. When the wind changed at Charlton Park, the residents had black smoke blowing into their windows instead of across the airfield. Even small draughts can cause problems. When lighting cameraman Peter Jessop wanted to create the tobacco-fume-laden atmosphere of the pilot's hut at Friston, the draught around the window frames sucked the smoke straight out of the tiny building. As large quantities of smoke are needed before the least haze shows up on film, the hut had to be filled to choking point. The camera crew were pleased to be reassured that the smoke was non-toxic.

For creating minor explosions, the favoured material is 'Cortex', a type of fuse cord designed for exploding gelig-nite. Unlike gelignite, cortex is a 'soft' pyrotechnic, which can only be ignited electrically. 'It comes in rolls, rather like washing line,' Graham explains. 'You can burn it, skip with it, you could even use it as a washing line without any risk of it exploding.' On *Piece of Cake* cortex was used, to blow in windows and help create the effect of cannon fire on the ground.

If the explosion is supposed to be inside the building, the cortex is placed round the windowframe on the inside of the building so that it blows the window outwards. To create the effect of a bomb exploding outside the building – as we often had to do in *Piece of Cake* – the cortex is placed round the outside of the windowframe. When the pilots' hut at St Pierre had to be hit by

The stuff that dreams are made of. Gerard O'Hare (Moran) gets his mind off the war during lunchbreak. A double decker bus served as location dining room (Charlton Park).

Above *Lighting cameraman Peter Jessop communes with his light meter.*

Left *On the movie: Peter Jessop in transit.*

a runaway Spitfire, for instance, cortex was laid round the outside of the windowframe and a remote controlled camera was set up inside the hut. When the explosion was triggered, glass and wood were sent flying towards the lens.

Cannon or machine gun fire consists of a quick series of small explosions. The charges (consisting of cortex with another soft pyrotechnic called 'Specimen 6' which adds flash and flame to the explosion) are laid in the ground, covered by earth or cork, and each is connected by wire to a nail board, which is, quite simply, a piece of wood with a row of nails in it. The charges are set off in quick succession by running a metal striker, which is connected to a battery, down the row of nails.

Above The script called for the CO's office to be 'damaged'. The special effects team handled the task with enthusiasm.

Right Sorry, Jane! The art department's handiwork reaches for the sky.

These explosions are designed to be quite safe for bystanders, but they did cause a problem to one of the attacking aeroplanes. Nick Grace's Messerschmitt, passing just 20 feet above the ground, caught an upwardly mobile clod of earth on the leading edge of its wingtip. While the clod was not very large and not moving particularly fast, the wingtip hit it at over 200 mph and picked up a dent. The underside of the aircraft was splattered but unharmed.

An effect which had to be created in the studio was gunfire from the Spitfire's wing. The real Spitfires no longer carry working machine guns and cannon. Film-makers sometimes fit aircraft with red strobe lights, but the results are seldom very good, so producer Andrew Holmes used two techniques to simulate gunfire in *Piece of Cake*.

The first technique was used for shots which showed the pilot's view as he looked out from his cockpit. It involved building a replica Spitfire wing, which was rigged in the studio at Elstree. The guns in the wing were loaded with a detonator and a small explosive charge. The camera was run as the charge was ignited. The camera was then cut and locked off so that it could not move at all while the guns were reloaded. The operation was repeated many times so that the final result on film was a series of explosions which, speeded up, created a continuous stream of gunfire.

We also needed to show gunfire coming from real flying aircraft. This effect was created in the videotape editing studio with the help of Paintbox

and Harry, which are computerised graphics and animation systems. The shots of the flying aircraft had been telecined (transferred from film on to digital videotape). The gunflashes were drawn on Paintbox and stored on disc. The Harry system was then used to retrieve and animate the flashes and ensure that they tracked across the frame with the wing of the moving aircraft. It took weeks to complete.

When the airfield was strafed by Messerschmitts, Graham's team had to create the effect of bullets hitting the side of a Spitfire. The fibreglass 'Trundler' replica Spitfire was the chosen victim. As an explosion in fibreglass would make an uneven shaped hole, a section of the fuselage was cut out and replaced with an aluminium sheet. Detonators were placed behind the plate; when they were set off they made the right kind of bullet-like hole in the side of the

Left *Simon Werry filming from the B25 rear gun position.*

Below *Special effects chief Graham Longhurst decorated his vehicle with a record of his 'kills'. The swastika represents Nick Grace's Messerschmitt.*

aircraft. The problem with the shot was getting the detonators in the 'Trundler' to appear at the same time and on the same line as the explosions on the ground.

Bombing raids on the airfield called for stronger stuff. Steel mortars containing a lifting charge were buried in the ground. The mortars are shaped like pyramids with their tops cut off; you bury them base upwards. Their tapered shape makes it easy to aim them slightly away from the camera and bystanders. Gelignite is often used as a lifting charge, but at Charlton Park 'ground maroons', containing black powder and flash powder, were used instead. The buried mortar is covered with bales of cork sheet, peat and fuller's earth, which are too light to cause too much damage to anyone if they are caught in the blast.

Sometimes there can be a slight discrepancy between what the director is expecting and what the special effects team think he is expecting. A scene shot at Friston called for Squadron Leader Barton's hut to be damaged in a raid. Director Ian Toynton was expecting to lose a window; special effects chief Longhurst thought he had

been briefed for something a little more dramatic. On the cue two mortars inside the hut blew off the roof and the whole structure collapsed like a cardboard cake box. 'Time for a rethink,' said Ian, toeing the wreckage.

While everyone enjoys seeing a building lift off like a rocket, special effects which involve the precious bodies of the cast need extremely careful planning. Technically, too, they are the most challenging.

Some of the most dramatic and horrifying scenes in *Piece of Cake* occur when characters are shot. When Squadron Leader Rex dies, for instance, we see bullets ripping through his jacket from behind: a scene that was intended to be frightening and unexpected. It was achieved by attaching 2–inch square metal plates inside Tim Woodward's flying jacket. On top of each plate was a sachet of 'Kensington Gore' (artificial blood) and in front of that was a small, electrically-fired detonator. The thick leather of the Irving jacket had been rubbed down with sandpaper to make it tissue thin. To protect the actor, a wad of foam rubber on a felt pad had been placed between his body and the back of the metal plates. On the cue the detonators blew holes through the leather and the shock wave from the explosion rebounded from the metal plates, bursting the sachets of blood and projecting the contents through the holes in the jacket.

Good timing is essential to get the best from effects like this. If the audience is to be surprised, the actor should not look as if he knows what is about to happen. If he jumps, the audience will jump. So although it might have been easier to give the actors a switch to trigger the explosions themselves, the director had them

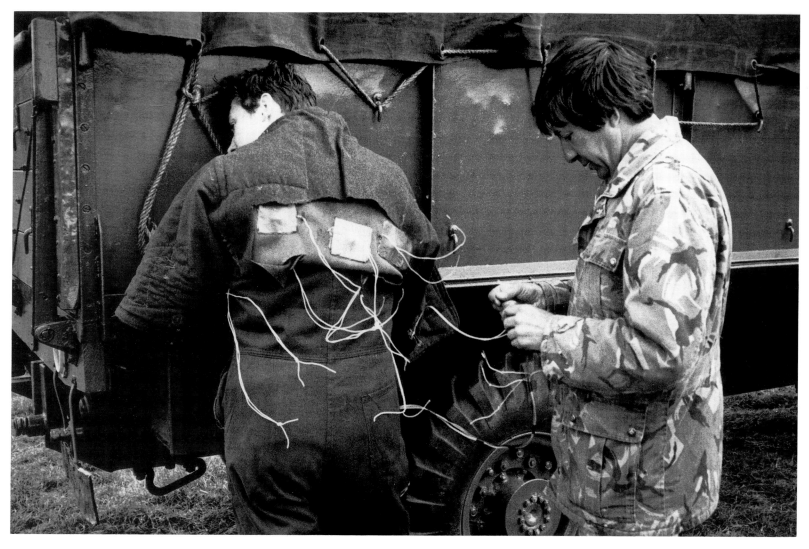

Above *Getting ready to be shot*

Opposite *David Horovitch as Kellaway.*

triggered remotely. He would cue the effect by some prearranged signal, like scratching his ear, so that the actor was unaware it was about to happen.

'Events like this should never be predictable,' director Toynton points out. 'You have to maintain the pace by constantly feeding the audience new information. On the other hand, when the audience knows that an event is going to happen, you have to make them wait for it.'

When the big raid was about to be launched on the château, the audience had been lulled into a false sense of security. Instead of waiting anxiously for the expected attack, the pilots were celebrating a wedding. Then the action struck very suddenly and very hard. 'I wanted to surprise the actors as well as the audience,' says Toynton. 'I had made the room look full by filling the back of the scene with stunt artists. All the actors knew was that the explosion would occur sometime during the song they were singing – but the song lasted three minutes and the explosion could occur at any moment during those three minutes. And they did not know exactly what kind of explosion to expect. I think it worked well; the shock on their faces is real.'

Flying the Messerschmitt Me 109

Walther Eichorn, a Lufthansa DC-10 pilot, is one of the few German aviators who can still claim to fly the Me 109. He flew Hans Dittes' Spanish built version of the aircraft over to England for *Piece of Cake*. In his spare time he is also one of Germany's most popular display pilots, flying the 109 and his own Harvard at airshows all over Europe.

This account first appeared, in a slightly longer form, in Warbirds Worldwide, *Issue No. 2, 1987.*

It was through flying the Harvard that I evenually met Hans Dittes and came to fly the Hispano *Buchon*; considered by many to be a 'Merlin engined 109'.

At this stage I had about 10,000 flight hours, 600 of them on taildraggers – 500 on Harvards. I had the Spanish HA-1112–M1L *Buchon* manual translated and Messerschmitt Bolkow Blohm Gmbh allowed me to view film of their rebuilt 109 during some of its flights including the one on which it crashed. It scared me a little, but it also made me realise that you have to be wide awake all the time you are at the controls of the *Buchon*. What helped most was an afternoon spent with Erich Hartmann – the Luftwaffe's leading 'Ace' with a staggering 352 confirmed victories during World War II.

Hans finally telephoned to tell me that the aircraft was ready for test flying in the autumn of 1986. The first day was spent ground running the Merlin 500, and taxying the aircraft all over the airfield to get the feel of its ground handling characteristics; something the *Buchon* is renowned for (it bites badly). The following day we did some high speed runs and then two days later the temporary flying permit arrived along with my licence including an 'Me 109' type rating.

The next morning I took my Harvard down to Mannheim, made one take off and landing there and one at Speyer (20nm miles South of Mannheim) as I was to ferry the *Buchon* there. After having prepared myself for the first flight I sat in the aircraft, closed the hood (it is very different to a sliding canopy) fired up the Merlin, taxied into position and concentrated on getting the aircraft airborne. Run up, and after about a 600 metre ground run we were airborne. Mannheim has a 900m long grass runway and I would have liked to have had an extra 100m available but with 12–15 knots wind on the nose it made up for the difference.

After getting airborne I retracted the gear, set the climb power to 2,650rpm, speed 300km/h and climbed to a safe altitude of 5,000 feet. Here I did approximately 30 minutes of general handling, including stalls in the landing configuration, simulated landings and go-arounds and gradually worked my way over to Speyer where I made my first landing after a 40 minute first flight.

Since then I have about 40 hours flight time on the aircraft with 60 take-offs and landings. Now you ask, how does he fly?

Why he? Well, my middle name is Fritz and the aircraft's German civil registration is D-FEHD: D (for *Deutschsland*), F (for *Fritz*), E (for *Eichorn*), H (for *Hans*) and D (for *Dittes*)! We call the aircraft *Fritz*! Now to the more serious aspects of *Fritz*. I have listed some points that pilots new to the notorious *Buchon* may find helpful to consider.

First of all the tight cockpit takes some getting used to. It is a good idea just to sit in the aircraft with the hood closed. The visibility from the cockpit is very poor, so S-turn during taxying more than other tail draggers. Secondly it is a good idea to think about the narrow gear, small rudder, and lots of power up front prior to every take-off. Consider also the cross-wind component which should be no more than five knots during your transition on to type; even now I do not like more than ten knots.

I personally recommend NO flaps for take-off because you can get airborne sooner with flaps but you may not be able to exercise control of the aircraft properly. Initially, keep the tail on the ground, until you reach a speed of approximately 100km/h then bring the tail up slowly, keep the aircraft straight, and if the rudder control is not sufficient ease back the power slightly. Now accelerate to around 180km/h (tail up) and just fly the aircraft off the ground. Watch the starboard wing, for it

will want to come up; a little right aileron will prevent that. If at all possible I would suggest initial flights be made off grass runways, because on this surface you can drift sideways – on concrete this will create a turn or swing and a classic ground loop situation. In addition to this the effect of inadvertantly applying brakes is not as disastrous on grass.

Once in the air the aircraft handles very nicely once you are used to the restricted visibility, up to around 450km/h. Thereafter the stick gets fairly stiff, mainly on the elevator and above 500km/h I have sometimes used both hands in a steep pull up.

For the landing; Slow down to under 300km/h, gear down, prop to 2,650rpm, slow to under 250km/h, lower flaps (full), open cowl flaps and aim to turn finals around 220km/h, slowing to 200km/h and eventually to 180km/h over the threshold. Landing is a

normal power-off over threshold and a three point landing. For the last portion of the approach it really helps to know in advance what obstacles to expect because the forward vision in landing is very poor. You can simulate it very well in the rear seat of a Harvard. It is a good idea to 'feel at home' in a Harvard before you even think about climbing into a 109 or *Buchon*.

Fritz and I have become good friends now and it is fun to zoom around with him when you are close to the deck at 600km/h (330kts) it feels almost like flying in an F-104 Starfighter at 450kts at 500 feet!

Flying the Spitfire – *a pilot's account*

Brian Smith was one of the team of pilots who flew Spitfires for *Piece of Cake*. He earns his living as a Boeing 757 captain with Air Europe; in his spare time he teaches aerobatics and flies a lightweight home-built racer.

He got his first chance to fly a Spitfire when Ray Hanna was short of a pilot to take three of the Old Flying Machine Company's aircraft to an airshow. This is his account of how he was checked out for his first solo in the Spit.

This account first appeared, in a slightly longer form, in Pilot *magazine, July 1988.*

The checkout process was split into two parts: first a couple of circuits flying a Harvard from the back seat to give some idea of the visibility problems of the real thing; and having sorted that out, a comprehensive briefing on the Spitfire followed by a thirty-minute familiarisation sortie. For once the weather was near perfect, with scattered cumulus, unlimited visibility and a fresh breeze down Duxford's runway. The Harvard trip went well enough considering I hadn't flown one since the mid-seventies – and then from the front seat! Flying from the back, with Ray in the front keeping an eye on the proceedings, produced few problems and certainly brought the visibility factor to the fore. Ironically, having spent years trying to encourage prospective Tiger Moth pilots to pull the stick back to attain the correct three-point attitude for landing, I ended up falling into the same trap in the Harvard. But the arrivals were close enough to three-pointers for 'the boss' to call it a day and head for the Spitfire.

If you are used to a Cessna 150 or similar, then your first impression of the Spitfire is of a big aeroplane. The natural lines of the fuselage tend to accentuate the aircraft's length, but the long nose forward of the leading edge contains nothing but engine.

Once seated on the inevitable parachute pack, two things become immediately apparent. The first is the lack of a cockpit floor, which exposes the fuselage frames and plumbing as well as the control runs, so woe betide you if you drop the odd pencil during a ferry transit. The second feature is the seemingly endless nose stretching out ahead – and not only is it long but surprisingly wide, courtesy of the Merlin's V-section.

To the modern eye the cockpit layout is haphazard, but after the initial shock it becomes relatively simple to get a grip on where everything is. Rudder and aileron trim wheels are mounted adjacent to the throttle quadrant on the left side; the latter also houses the mixture and pitch controls. Below this are a small selection of switches, the only one of any major importance controlling the radiator doors. The instrument panel contains the basic T layout, with airframe information such as brake/pneumatic pressure and trim position indicators grouped on the left of the panel, and instrumentation for the engine and fuel system set on the right. One incongruous switch that can easily be missed is the flap selector, which lives at the top left corner of the panel. With only two positions available to the pilot – *up* or *down* – there seems little need for refinement in this area. Fuel and starter/ignition controls are mounted along the bottom of the panel, with the right side of the cockpit dominated by the undercarriage selector, an extremely cumbersome looking device given the fragile appearance of the gear.

The seating arrangements allow for any shape and size of pilot, with the seat adjustable in height and the rudder pedals for leg length. The first thing that needs to be done is to set the brakes, which involves opening the pneumatic shutoff valve by your left elbow and then setting the bicycle-type brake lever on the stick.

The process is accompanied by much hissing of air as the lines pressurise, which confirms the fact that you are dealing with an aeroplane that runs on systems. Engine starting requires a degree of fuel pressure to be established via the pump on the right cockpit side. Having applied about thirty cycles, the next item on the agenda is the primer, which requires half-a-dozen shots into a cold engine.

The throttle is set around an inch open, the stick is held firmly back and the starter and ignition booster buttons are pressed simultaneously. Once the engine fires the ignition switches are selected *on* (they live just forward of the throttle quadrant), and with any luck you are in business. The process is a bit more complicated when the engine is hot, and care needs to be taken to avoid over-priming, lest sheets of flame erupt from the exhaust stacks.

Having got the engine going, time is of the essence to get out to the holding point; the cooling system is designed to work when airborne, and even with the radiator flaps wide open there isn't much time to play with. Taxying needs to be conducted with caution; apart from the restricted visibility the castoring tailwheel allows the aeroplane to wander around, and it takes practice to get used to the brake lever on the spade grip which regulates the pneumatic brakes.

Once at the holding point the engine run-up is limited to around 1,800 rpm because of the lack of elevator authority. The only pre-take-off check item that is out of the ordinary is the application of full right rudder trim to counteract the torque.

The most striking sensation of the take-off is the *noise*! Twelve stub exhausts are less than ten feet ahead, with only the thickness of the perspex providing any sort of sound barrier. Despite the capacity of the Merlin, take-off rpm is in the order of 2,900. The throttle is taken to the gate half way up the quadrant, which provides around plus twelve pounds of boost; any more starts to cause embarrassment with the torque effect. Acceleration is on a par with a modern aerobatic aircraft like the Pitts Special – not surprising given the similarity in the power to weight ratio, and is accompanied by a definite tendency to head for the left side of the runway. Gentle forward pressure on the stick is needed to raise the tail, and with the elevator trim set slightly aft of neutral the aeroplane flies itself off the runway at less than sixty knots. Once established in the climb a hand-swapping exercise is required to raise the gear via the selector on the right side of the cockpit. The operation of the selector requires three separate actions, that is, out of the *down* gate, raised to the *up* gate and then ensure that the lever (as well as the gear) is mechanically locked and the hydraulic system off-loaded.

Having sorted that out, the power can be adjusted to around 2,700 rpm and plus eight for the climb, which is best flown at 120 knots.

The final item on the agenda is to remember to select the radiator cowls to *auto*.

It seems to take no time at all to get up to a sensible cruising height. The aircraft settles down to a comfortable 200 knots at a power setting of 2,000 rpm and plus four. The visibility in the flying attitude is much improved, although the canopy arch and gunsight still provide some restrictions. The elevators and rudder are quite light and can be trimmed out to fly hands and feet off, although the machine is slightly unstable in pitch – something that was never quite sorted out by the designers. In contrast the ailerons are comparatively heavy, but to some extent this is due to the spade grip configuration of the stick which requires most of the effort to come from the pilot's wrist rather than his arm. The early marks of Spitfire certainly suffered from this problem, and matters were improved by changing to metal rather than fabric-covered control surfaces.

But these comments are nitpicking. The machine is basically a joy to fly, and will turn on a sixpence without causing any undue problems. There is ample natural warning from the wing of an impending stall, and all that is required is a minor decrease in back pressure on the stick for the situation to resolve itself.

The design of the wing achieved a superb balance between plenty of lift without excessive induced drag, and with the comparatively low wing loading (around 25 pounds per square foot) there are few, if any, comparable aircraft that could see a Spitfire off in a turning fight. Aerobatics are simplicity itself, thanks to the constant-speed propeller. At 2,700 rpm and plus eight the aircraft can be flown through the classic figures, including half vertical rolls, without putting any undue stress on the airframe. Entry speeds are in the order of 250 knots, although once familiar with the aeroplane looping figures can be flown from 200 knots with care. These sort of speeds allow the machine to be manoeuvred in a comparatively small space – especially important in the context of airshow flying. Formation flying produces an unusual effect of the aeroplane moving laterally if significant throttle movements are made – another by-product of the engine torque. The other factor that needs consideration is the sheer weight of the aeroplane. This is not a Tiger Moth or Cessna 150, but around three tons of very powerful machinery moving at considerable speed; therefore forethought is always required in

terms of where to point the nose.

As mentioned, the wing gives plenty of natural warning prior to the stall. The aircraft stalls at seventy knots clean, or ten knots less with gear and flaps lowered. The break at the stall is marked, with elevator control still available, and in this case, no wing drop.

With these characteristics the approach and landing phase can be flown with confidence. Lowering the flaps produces a marked pitch-down trim change – not surprising because of their all-or-nothing design. The rate of descent is very high with a glide approach, so a touch of power helps in this respect. A curved pattern at around 75 knots needs to be flown during the approach to maintain reasonably forward visibility, which reduces to virtually zero in the flare. Speed loss in the flare is quite dramatic, with touchdown in the three-point attitude similar in technique to a Tiger Moth; and once on the ground the rollout requires some effort with the rudder, especially in a crosswind. In such circumstances it is better to accept the wind from the right, thereby playing the wind against the torque should a bit of propwash be needed. As far as landing distance is concerned, a 500 metre strip is quite adequate for someone familiar with the aeroplane.

The memory of that first flight in the Spitfire ranks alongside my first faltering solo in a Tiger many years ago. Looking back on the experience it was with a degree of terror – of the size and power of the aircraft as well as what Ray would do to me if I bent it! Subsequently, both pilot and aeroplane have flown shows from the haunting remoteness of Norway to the timeless beauty of the Swiss Alps.

The more you get to know the machine the greater your appreciation of Mitchell's design becomes, and the aircraft's flying qualities cetainly endorse the respect of all those pilots who went to war in her. It is certainly a humbling experience to have the opportunity to fly the Spitfire – to be one of the very lucky few.

Piece of Cake kept quite a few people busy during the spring and summer of 1988. Here are some of them:

PIECE OF CAKE

Cast

Rex	Tim Woodward
Kellaway	David Horovitch
Skelton	Richard Hope
Barton	Tom Burlinson
Cattermole	Neil Dudgeon
Hart	Boyd Gaines
Bletchley	Michael Elwyn
Stickwell	Gordon Lovitt
Starr	Tom Radcliffe
Moran	Gerard O'Hare
Patterson	George Anton
Fitzgerald	Jeremy Northam
Gordon	Nat Parker
Cox	Patrick Bailey
Miller	Mark Womack
Lloyd	Timothy Lyn
Trevelyan	Jason Calder
Ramsay	Jack McKenzie
Dutton	Sam Miller
Marriott	Stephen MacKenna
Steele Stebbing	Julian Gartside
Zadarnowski	Tomek Bork
Haducek	Ned Vukovic
Hubbard	Christopher Godwin
Spencer	Adrian Ross Magenty
Wing Co. Ashe	Brian Ralph
McFarlane	Simon Adams
Renouf	Jonathan Dow
Brooke	Adam Armstrong
Rochard	Gerad Cherqui
Martineau	Les Clack
Delacroix	Bud Breckon
Mary	Helena Michell
Nicole	Corinne Dacla
LAC Todd	Neil Clark
Gullet	John Bleasdale
Airman accordionist	Marcel Dupont
Drummer	Bobby Armstrong
Bass	Pete Morgan
Dower	Ellis Jones
Benson	Nick Bartlett
Flt Sergeants	Ian Flintoff
	Jeremy Browne
Control Corporal	Richard Hague
Airman	Angus Kennedy
Despatch rider	Steve Fletcher
Fitter	Niall Sutherland
Armourer	Peter Attard
Padre	Richard Brain
Chaplain	Tony Crean
Doctor	Richard Durden
Corporal King	Colin Dunn
French priest	Olivier Pierre
Henri	Daniel Pageon
Mr Burnett	Vass Anderson
Mrs Burnett	Angela Wyndham Lewis
Mr Ellis	Martin Matthews
Frenchman	Lawrence Davidson
Singer	Elma Soiron
Landlord	Gordon Salkild
Simpson	Jonathan Evans
German soldier	Fergus McLarnon
French farmer	Geoffrey Greenhill
Chef	Chris MacDonnell
Mayor	Claude Le Sache
Reilly the dog	Toby

Production

Executive producer	Linda Agran
Producer	Andrew Holmes
Director	Ian Toynton
Associate producer	Adrian Bate
Script writer	Leon Griffiths
Author	Derek Robinson
Series administrator	Stephen Taylor
Production manager/ 1st assistant director	Jake Wright
Production co-ordinator	Caroline Cornish-Trestrail
2nd assistant director	Paul Frift
3rd assistant director	Tom Harvey
Location managers	Michael Hook
	Nigel Gostelow
Script supervisor	Julie Robinson
Production assistant	Jenny Mauthe
Producer's secretary	Gaynor Wilson
	Ailsa Robbie
Production runners	Philip Kitcher
	Jamie Byng
	Luke Dunkley
Jobfit trainee	Lindsey Bleach

Cameras

Lighting cameraman	Peter Jessop
Camera operator	John Maskall
Focus puller	David Morgan
Clapper/loader	Jonathan Earp
Grip	John Etherington

Aerial unit

Aerial cameraman	Simon Werry
2nd aerial cameraman	Jeff Mulligan
Clapper/loader	Tim Potter
Camera assistant	Stephen Brooke Smith
Camera mounts	Peter Thomson
plus	Chris Lovegrove
	Peter Ditch
	Ray Moore
	Lee Gold
	Ray Mayfield
	Dave Atkinson
	John Fletcher
	Richard Brierley
	Jamie Harcourt
	John Fletcher
	Bill Pochetty
	Ian Horn
	John Beeden

Camera Supplier

	Sidney Samuelson
	Simon Broad

Sound

Sound recordist	Colin Nicolson
Boom operator	Rupert Castle
Sound engineer	Tony Cook

Flying

Associate producer	Robert Eagle
Chief pilot	Ray Hanna
Deputy chief pilot	Mark Hanna
Spitfire pilots	Stephen Grey
	Peter Jarvis
	Hoof Proudfoot
	Carl Schofield
	Brian Smith
	John Watts
	Howard Pardue (USA)
Messerschmitt pilots	Nick Grace
	Reg Hallam
	Walther Eichorn
B25 pilots	Vernon Thorp
	Anita Mays
	Jack Skipper (USA)
	Walter Wootton (USA)
Harvard pilot	John Romaine
Junkers pilot	Peter Hoare
Helicopter pilot	Michael Malric Smith (Castleair)
Aircraft engineers	Roger Shepherd
	Mick Sheahan
	Ray Thomas
	Paul Kiddell
	Lawrence Laveris
Helicopter engineers	Mike Wight
	John Souch
	Simon Pettit
Timekeeper	Patsy Davidson
Technical advisors	Peter Matthews
	Philip Congdon
Firemen	David Arnold
	Chris Spiers
	John Brownlee

Peter Webber
Howard Dwyer
Hamish Ross
Roddie Gunn
John Miller
Jim Wallace

Bowser driver   Ray Smith

Replica Spitfires

Alan Brown
Brent Johnson
Sheena Feggans
Richard Brown
Derek Johnson
David Brighton
Martin Gaskell
Walter Ironside
Paul Hoffman
Bernard Ware

Casting
Casting director   Marilyn Johnson
Vini Liffe (USA)
Susie Maizels
(Australia)
Laura Johnson

Art department
Art director   Jane Coleman
Asst art director   Peter Wenham
Props buyer   Judy Farr
Art department
runners   Matthew Dirkan

Props
Property master   Dave Newton
Paul Turner
Colin Burgess
Brian Aldridge
Mike Smith

Construction
Construction
manager   Tom Marsh
Vincent Burk
Peter Mousey

plus   Michael Redmond
Bill Keenan
Reg Lockwood

Electricians
Gaffer   John Donaghue
Best boy   Warren Ewen
Generator
operator   Reg Pape

Electrician   Roy Branch

Special effects
Supervisor   Graham
Longhurst
Dominic Tuohy
Peter Arnold
Ian Biggs

Wardrobe
Costume
designer   Lynette Cummin
Asst designer   Michael Price
Annie Crawford
Joe Hobbs

Make-up
Supervisor   Beryl Lerman
Make up artist   Linda Armstrong
Magdalen Gaffney

Hair
Helen Lennox
Stephanie Kaye
Victoria Lennox

Accountants
Production
accountants   Nuala Alen-
Buckley
Irene Jay

Accounts
manager   Marilyn Freeman

Editing
Editors   Roger Wilson
Barry Peters
Assembly editor   David Gasson
1st asst editor   Sue Dempsey
2nd asst editor   Jonathan Enright
Mooney
Asst editor   Sean Mackenzie
Dubbing editor   Colin Chapman
Dialogue editor   Brigitte Arnold
Jobfit trainee   Kishor Patel

Stunts
Stunt arranger   Alf Joint
Tracy Eddon
Sarah Franzl
Nick Hobbs
Steve Dent
Steve Street
Tim Lawrence
Ginger Keane
Pat Slattery

Animal trainers
Pauline Clift
Walter Mew

Publicity
Press   Wanda Rumney
Zoe McIntyre
Shane Chapman

Stills
photographers   Simon Farrell
Tony Russell
Mike Vaughan

Aerial and production stills photography
Herbie Knott

Transport
Phil Knight
Michael Marks
Peter Kyriacou
Gary Palmer
Brian Baverstock
David Snow
Bob Allen
Jimmy Derby
Paul Bates
Roy Osborn
Neil Brown
Laurie Fowles
George Roberts

Action vehicles
Michael Rickaby
Rodney Rymell
Robin Rymell
John Simomson
John Boys

Catering
Sally Spratt
Mark Soar
Kirsty Ainslie
Ken Clarkspon
Nikki Walker

Elstree studios
Andrew Mitchell
John Shepherd
Wendy Smith
April Small
Colin Wilson

Laboratories
Len Brown
Rick Nowak
Clive Noakes

Sound dubbing
Steve Turner

Telecine and videotape editing
Brian Wiseman
Alan Kaye
Colin Reynolds
Phil Price
Roy Beck
Simon Brewster
Al Hayes
Peter Astor
Simon Maxwell
Jim Mullion

Location facilities
Ron Lowe
Tony Bird
Alison Morrow

With special thanks to the officers and men of the Royal Corps of Transport at the Duke of Gloucester Barracks, South Cerney.

AN AIRMAN'S ECSTASY

Oh, I have slipped the surly bonds of earth
And danced the skies on laughter-silvered
  Wings:
Sunward I've climbed, and joined the
  tumbling mirth
Of sun-split clouds – and done
  a hundred things
You have not dreamed of: wheeled and
  soared and swung
High in the sunlit silence. Hovering there
I've chased the shouting wind along, and
  flung
My eager craft through footless halls of air;
Up, up the long delirious, burning blue
I've topped the wind-swept heights with easy
  grace,
Where never lark nor even eagle flew;
And while, with silent lifting mind I've trod
The high, untrespassed sanctity of space,
Put out my hand, and touched the face of
  God.

This poem was written by Pilot Officer J. G. Magee of the
Royal Canadian Air Force shortly before his death.

118

Acknowledgements

This book was written and edited while *Piece of Cake* was still in production. I would like to thank everyone on the production team and cast who gave me their time during a very busy period, especially Ian Toynton, Adrian Bate and Andrew Holmes.

ROBERT EAGLE

My thanks to Neil Grimshaw at FUJI PHOTO FILM UK LTD and Sue Colman at NIKON UK LTD for kindly supplying film and specialist camera equipment. Simon Werry at Market Films for technical assistance. Alun John, Mike Spillard, Frances Cutler, Sarah Heneghan, John Luff, Peter Gillard & Stewart Goldstein at The *Independent* for their support and encouragement. Sarah Mahaffy at Boxtree for her unwavering backing for the project. And, lastly, to Keith Smith, former Picture Editor of *The Times*, to whom so many of us owe our careers.

HERBIE KNOTT